THE ULTIMATE GUIDE
TO BREAKING INTO
TECH SALES

THE ULTIMATE GUIDE TO BREAKING INTO

TECH

SALES

LAND YOUR DREAM JOB,

MAKE SIX FIGURES,

& WORK FROM ANYWHERE

BRANDON BORNANCIN

WWW.SEAMLESS.AI

Tech sales is the greatest job in the world.

If you can learn how to sell in tech, you can do anything.

My mission with this book is to help over 1,000,000 people get a job in tech sales.

Let's make it happen...

Good luck!

CONTENTS

ABOUT BRANDON BORNANCIN
WWW.BRANDONBORNANCIN.COM

Brandon Bornancin is the founder and CEO of Seamless.AI – The world's best sales leads software, three-time bestselling author of *Whatever It Takes, Sales Secrets,* and *Seven Figure Social Selling,* podcast host of *Sales Secrets,* and one of the most influential motivational speakers in the world. He's on a mission to help 1,000,000 people make over $1,000,000 by connecting the world to opportunity and positively impacting billions.

Growing up as a poor kid from Ohio, Brandon got his first job as a janitor. He knew at an early age, there had to be a better way of life. Brandon then decided to get into tech sales and launch his first company at 18 which generated over $12M in sales. After that, he sold over $100M for Google and IBM. Quickly thereafter he launched the #1 sales leads software in the U.S. called Seamless.AI, valued at over $1 Billion in just 4 years. He became a millionaire in his twenties, worth over $100,000,000 in his thirties, and he's just getting started. His strong work ethic, positive attitude, and whatever it takes mindset have empowered him to go all in on helping others maximize their full potential.

Contact Brandon for speaking engagements, podcast interviews, products, or questions at:

www.BrandonBornancin.com

- **Seamless.AI:** Brandon Bornancin is the founder & CEO of Seamless. AI – The World's Best Sales Leads. Seamless.AI finds cell phones, emails, and direct dials for anyone in seconds using artificial intelligence. The company helps over 300,000 salespeople, entrepreneurs, and marketers globally. His customers have generated an estimated

15.34 million new appointments, 3.06 million new deals, and over $29 Billion in sales. Seamless is celebrated by millions of fans for helping over 16,000 salespeople make over $100,000 in sales, and over 5,000 salespeople make over $1,000,000 in sales. Join Seamless for free at:

www.seamless.ai

- **We Are Hiring:** Seamless.AI has consistently won "Best Places to Work" awards, including being named one of the "Top 10 Startups" by LinkedIn, the "#1 SaaS Company in the Midwest" by Forbes Magazine, and the "#1 Tech Company of the Year." Our people fuel our success, and that's why we have over 500 sales positions open right now. 425 Sales Development Rep (SDR) positions, 200 Account Executive (AE) positions, and hundreds of others. Apply to join us at:

www.seamless.ai/about/careers

- **Books:** Brandon is an international bestselling author of three books including *Whatever It Takes: Master the Habits to Transform Your Business, Relationships, and Life, Sales Secrets: The World's Top Sales Experts Share Their Secrets to Success*, and *Seven Figure Social Selling: Over 400 Pages of Proven Social Selling Scripts, Strategies, and Secrets to Increase Sales and Make More Money Today!* Get his books on Amazon here:

www.amzn.to/3W4Ssg2

- **Podcast:** Brandon is the host of the #1 sales podcast, *Sales Secrets*, where he interviews the world's best sales experts on their top secrets to success. Podcast guests and interviews include Gary Vaynerchuk, *Shark Tank* star, Kevin Harrington, "Mr. 10x," Grant Cardone, "Wolf of Wall Street," Jordan Belfort, Tom Bilyeu from *Impact Theory*, Ryan Serhant from Bravo's *Million Dollar Listing*, Daymond John, Jeb Blount, Anthony Iannarino, Jill Konrath, and many more! Request Brandon to join your podcast for free or pitch yourself to be on his show at:

www.BrandonBornancin.com/podcast

- **Awards:** Brandon Bornancin and his team have won many awards most recently: "LinkedIn's Top 10 Startups," "#1 Bestselling Book Award" for *Whatever It Takes*, "#1 Best Places to Work," "#1 Tech Company of the Year," "#1 Bestselling Book Award" for *Sales Secrets*, "#1 Best Remote Places to Work," "#1 Tech Company in the Midwest" by Forbes, Salesforce.com's "Top Sales Expert," "#1 Bestselling Book Award" for *Seven Figure Social Selling*, InsideSales.com's "#1 Sales Leader," and many more. Check out our latest wins here:

www.BrandonBornancin.com/awards

- **Speaker:** Brandon is an award-winning national public speaker delivering famous keynotes and speaker presentations at events like Dreamforce, Outbound, Demo Day, SaaStr, SXSW, Sundance, and many others. He shares his story with Fortune 500 companies, professional sports teams, high-growth startups, sales teams, entrepreneur organizations, private equity portfolios, associations, and hundreds of thousands of people across the country. Request Brandon to speak at your next event at:

www.BrandonBornancin.com/speaking

- **Press:** Brandon is recognized as one of the top salespeople and technology entrepreneurs in the world. He is frequently featured in Forbes, The Wall Street Journal, Fortune, ABC, Yahoo News, The Nasdaq, LinkedIn Top Startups, The New York Times, Entrepreneur. com, CNN, Business Insider, WBNS, #1 Best Places to Work, and many others. For TV, press, or story inquiries, contact Brandon at:

www.BrandonBornancin.com/press

- **Startup Investing:** Brandon is an early-stage angel investor, venture capitalist, technology investor, and sales advisor (Seamless.AI, Facebook, Twitter, Uber, Slack, Snapchat, and 25+ others). If you are a startup looking for VC, angel investing, or private equity funding, contact him. If you are a startup looking for advisors or board members, he also advises companies for 0.1% - 5% equity depending on the stage, growth, and size of business. Contact him at:

www.BrandonBornancin.com

- **Real Estate Investing:** Brandon is an avid real estate investor. His current portfolio is worth tens of millions with aspirations to scale to $100 Million and $1 Billion. If you have multi-family real estate investment opportunities, please contact him at:

www.BrandonBornancin.com

- **Community & Giving Back:** Brandon Bornancin is heavily involved in the community. Brandon and his wife help spread awareness for whole food, plant-powered living to support the fight against Alzheimer's disease, cancer, heart disease, diabetes, and many others. He lost his mother to Alzheimer's disease when he was in college and believes the food we eat can prevent the world's deadliest diseases. Additionally growing up in a family that struggled financially to buy essentials like clothing and food, Brandon and his wife work to donate as much money and time as possible to several charities.

- **Hobbies:** Brandon likes to work out, read, and surf in his free time. Brandon and his wife also love traveling to the East Coast during the summer, or surfing oceanside during the winter!

We Are Hiring

Seamless.AI has over 500 open sales positions.
Apply Today at Seamless.AI/Careers!

Join Our Team

seamless.AI/careers

Apply Now

PART 1

THE SECRET

THE #1 SECRET TO SUCCESS THAT NO ONE EVER TELLS YOU

Do you ever see people get ahead of you who are less talented, less hard-working, less capable, or less intelligent?

- They get the job over you.

- They make more money than you.

- They get the promotions and raises over you.

- They get the cars and houses over you.

- They get to date the person of their dreams over you.

Does it constantly feel like it's happening all the time around you?

Your friends are winning. Your co-workers are winning. Your family is winning.

And no matter what you do or what you try… you just can't take your wealth, health, work, relationships, or success to the next level?

I totally get it. It's frustrating, I know.

This is something I used to experience all the time.

I knew I had massive potential and talent.

I'd work super hard and go all out… But no matter what, I just couldn't figure out how to get ahead of the pack.

I couldn't figure out why no matter how hard I worked, other people were getting ahead while I was being left behind in the dust.

That's until I finally figured out the secret to success in both business and life…

I was traveling for one of my first new sales jobs, and I'd spent a few days out on the West Coast for sales meetings (getting to travel like this to meet with new prospective companies to sell to is one of the many amazing benefits of working in sales).

I was in line to board a flight that was supposed to be heading home when out of nowhere the flight attendant informed us that our flight had been canceled.

It was 9:30 PM, and we would have to reschedule a flight for the next day to head back to Columbus, Ohio.

Other than the obvious inconvenience of having a canceled flight (no one likes those), there was one, urgent issue I had to fix…

I had to make it back ASAP for one of the largest deals I was pitching to close the next day.

If I could win this deal, it would cover all my expenses for months and put me in the #1 sales spot for the quarter at my company.

I worked on this deal for over six months with a dozen people at my company, and we invested thousands of dollars in pitch prep.

Flying out the next day was not going to be an option for me.

Now, I could have taken two different routes here…

With the first route, I could have taken the L, like everyone else did on the flight, flown out the next day, and missed winning one of the biggest deals of my career at the time.

I could have been one of the many people the airlines screwed over that day, and spent the night sleeping on the airport floor, just to get herded onto a sold-out flight the next day, completely cramped at the back of the plane next to the bathroom.

With the second route, I could refuse to accept the bad hand I'd just been dealt, and sell the flight attendant to get me on the earliest available flight out.

The first route sounded terrible, so instead of giving in, I went into WHATEVER IT TAKES mode.

I waited in a long line to speak to the attendant at the booth and started the conversation very politely (despite what you've heard, nice people don't finish last, they finish first).

I went up to her booth and I thanked her for all her hard work with our flight. Then I slowly went into building my business case with her. This is what I call sales pitch mode where you start covering needs, wants, goals, dreams, desires, and negotiating tactics – and you essentially influence the situation to go in your favor.

After five minutes of presenting my case and trying to sell her on the urgency of my situation…

She finally agreed with me and worked her magic on the computer. She made some calls and got me on another airline's flight that was leaving in the next 2 hours.

GAME ON!

I couldn't believe it!

I presented my sales pitch, made my case, and boom, she was sold.

Not only did the flight attendant find a flight scheduled for me to get home that night, but she was also able to bump me up to first class for free! When I got on that plane and sat down in my first class seat (which was the first time I had ever flown first class by the way), I just sat in awe at what I was able to do with a single pitch.

That's when it hit me, and I had one of the most life-changing epiphanies that transformed the trajectory of my life forever for the better.

I learned one of the most important secrets to success in business and in life.

Do you know what the secret is?

Think about it for a second…

Why did I get what I wanted in life while all the other people on that canceled flight had to spend the rest of their night sitting curled up on the floor at the airport?

The reason why I got onto the next flight out in an upgraded seat that same evening wasn't because I was smarter or more talented or more deserving than anyone else…

It was because I knew how to sell.

The #1 reason why people succeed over others is because they know how to sell better than you and better than the masses.

They understand that everything in life is a sale, and everything they get is a commission.

THE TOP 1% ARE ALL SALESPEOPLE

The vast majority of the most successful people in the world are salespeople, have a background in sales, or they spent a significant amount of their time mastering sales.

Don't believe me? Check this out.

There are 3,311 billionaires and over 62 million millionaires.

Only 10% of the 3,311 billionaires inherited their money from their families.

The rest are ultra-successful salespeople and entrepreneurs who had to sell something to someone every day to grow their business.

These billionaires and millionaires are selling their products, their company, their vision, and their ideas to someone else all the time.

Selling never ends for the ultra-wealthy and successful.

Why is this the case?

Why are there so many millionaires and billionaires who are salespeople?

It's because sales is the only job where you can go from broke to financially free the fastest, and do it with little to no professional education or experience.

I sincerely believe that sales is the best career in the world for this reason alone!

This is a career where you can become great at serving others, helping others, and selling others. And by perfecting this craft, you help people get everything they want in life and you in turn get everything you want in this life.

EVERYTHING IN LIFE IS A SALE

The secret to going from broke to financially free…

The secret to achieving everything you want in life…

The secret to having it all… the family, the money, the freedom, the time off, the houses, the cars, and the vacations…

The secret is SALES!

Whether you want to believe it or not, everything in life is a sale. And the quicker you master this secret to success, the quicker you will get everything you want in business and in life.

If you are great at sales, you will get your way and close the sale.

But if you are bad at sales, other people will get their way and close *you* on the sale.

Everything in life is a sale and sales isn't just an exchange of money.

Sales can be an exchange of ideas, solutions, agreements, or decisions.

Some of the greatest sales I've ever made had nothing to do with money and everything to do with sharing my point of view with someone and persuading them to agree with me.

One of the main reasons why people try but often fail in tech sales is because they don't get sold on why sales is the greatest job in the world, and they never truly grasp the core fundamentals that everything in life is a sale.

Here are some examples of different kinds of sales that are happening 24/7 to everyone around the world regardless of your professional or personal experience.

Even though these are everyday situations, your ability to sell always determines your level of success or failure in these scenarios.

EXAMPLES OF SALES BEING MADE EVERY DAY

Listed below are examples of of sales being made every day whether you know it or not.

- **Getting a raise:** No one is going to give you a raise or a promotion just because you want one. To get a raise, you need to sell the employer on why they should increase their budget and investment in you.

  I've hired thousands of people, and whenever an employee asks for a raise, I ask myself, "Are the results and impact far greater than what we are investing in them?"

  Your goal is to sell the employer on the results you've delivered in the past and the big impact your future actions will deliver. If you sell the manager on the value you provide, you get the raise. If not, you stay stuck at the same salary rate.

- **Growing your network with super wealthy, valuable contacts:** In order to connect with people who are richer and smarter than you, you need to sell them on investing their time in meeting with you. These people are in high demand and have no time to waste, so your ability to sell them on why they should meet with you is critical!

- **Picking a vacation spot:** If you want to go somewhere on vacation with your friends or family, you have to sell them on where you want to go and create the business case for why your location is ideal.

  Let's say you want to go to the Bahamas, but one of your friends wants to go to Lake Tahoe. Well, you'd better know how to pitch all the benefits of a trip to the Bahamas, otherwise, you're going to spend your spring break in Tahoe.

  If you go to the Bahamas, you sold your family or friends to go where you want to go. But if you are headed to Lake Tahoe, you lost the sale.

- **Getting someone to agree with you:** Let's say you're debating with someone and you're trying to convince them to not only admit they are wrong, but to also take your side. To make this happen, you need exceptional selling skills. You have to persuade them to be open-minded and then you have to present the evidence that closes them to agree with you. Getting anyone to take your side about anything is a sale.

If you master selling, then you can get anyone to agree with you in any situation.

- **Getting the table you want at a restaurant:** When you spend a lot of money to go out to eat at a nice restaurant, you want to have the best seat in the house.

  In order to get the best table at the restaurant, you have to sell the host on why they should seat you at your desired location vs. a table that is more convenient for them.

  This happens to me all the time, especially when going to restaurants on the water. I can get seated inside or outside by the ocean, and for whatever reason, the host always tries to sit my family in the back of the restaurant by the bathroom with no water view.

  Getting the table you want is a sale, and you have to close the host to get it.

- **Checking out late at a hotel**: Checking out late at a hotel is a sale. Imagine you are on vacation at one of the most amazing resorts in the world. The trip is coming to an end but your flight doesn't leave until the evening. Well, if you want to stay, you need to request a late checkout. The only problem is you are staying at a sold-out hotel. To sell the hotel on what you want, you will need to go up to the counter and sell them on why they should let you extend your stay a few hours.

  Those who can sell, get to enjoy their room in paradise for a few more hours. Those who can't sell leave paradise early and spend the day bored out of their mind at the airport!

Everything is a sale, even simple things like checking out of your hotel room late vs. early.

- **Entertainment:** Picking the entertainment you want is a sale.

  When my wife and I are headed to Vegas for entertainment, we are both building a list of shows we want to see. Once we have our list, we have to sell the pros, benefits, and value props of why one of our shows is better than the other and commit to going to see it.

  The entertainment you watch live, the tv shows, Netflix, you name it. It's all a sale!

  The creator of the show has to sell you to watch it. Then you have to sell your significant other or family to watch it over something else. It's all a sale.

- **Bank loans or credit cards:** When you go to the bank to get a credit card or a loan to buy a new car, this is a big sale. The bank reps will sell you on why you should go with them, and you will sell them on why they should give you a better interest rate for your loan or line of credit.

  The majority of bankers even get a commission for every loan that gets signed, so don't ever forget that... Every banker is a salesperson trying to sell you something, and you are always trying to sell the bank to give you a loan to buy at the lowest rate possible. Who is going to be the best salesperson? With this book, it's going to be you!

- **Skipping the line at the nightclub:** Skipping the line at a sold-out nightclub is a sale.

  Let's say it's Friday night. You're at the hottest club in town. And of course, there's a line down the street of people waiting to get in. Those who can sell, get to skip the line and have the time of their lives, dancing and having fun with their friends. Those who can't sell, spend the entire night waiting in line, only to be turned away because by the time they get to the front, the club closes. Getting into a VIP club is a sale.

- **Getting someone to go out with you:** Getting someone to go on a date with you is a sale. Let's say there is a guy or girl you've had a crush on forever and you want them to go out with you. Guess what? You have to sell them to say "Yes." If you sell that person, you get the date, and this could turn into future dates. Maybe this person ends up being your future wife or husband! I know because this happened to me after four years of chasing my dream girl. I finally sold her to say "Yes" and the rest is history (love you Danielle!).

If you don't sell that person, you don't get to go out with them and you possibly never will.

- **Getting a new job:** To get a new job, you have to sell yourself to the employer on all the value you can bring to the table if you joined the company.

You have to sell them through your resume, through your interview answers, through your appearance, and through your confidence. The company is then going to evaluate and weigh the potential impact you can make. As an employer, I almost always hire the person who sells me and convinces me that they're the perfect candidate for the job. They could just be starting in their field, but if they sell me on their work ethic and the returns they can deliver, I will pick them every day over someone with tons of experience but no sales skills.

- **Politicians are salespeople:** Politicians want to sell you on their vision to change the world so you'll give them your vote when elections come around. Politicians sell around the clock in their communities, on the news, at events, etc. If they win the election, they sold enough people to win the deal. If they don't get elected, their opponent turned out to be a better salesperson.

- **The news is always selling you:** My sister works for the news and I know for a fact that the news is trying to sell you all the time to pay attention to their story and stop scrolling through other tv stations. The news anchor will try to hook you with their story so you stop switching channels and tune in as long as possible to their news station.

This is also why news anchors always talk primarily about negative stories because pain sells more than success in the news. That being said, every news anchor is selling you sensation and pain to get your attention, which is the commission.

Everything is a sale... Open your eyes and you will see this fundamental truth.

- **Waking up early:** Getting up early to get ahead of the competition requires you to sell yourself on waking up when the alarm goes off (not hitting snooze for the 10th time), and getting started right away with attacking your to-do list, etc.

If you want to go from waking up at 10 AM to waking up at 5 AM, you have to sell and convince yourself that the benefits of starting your day early outweigh the pains.

- **Selling yourself to study:** As a student, you have to sell yourself to stay up all night to study for a final exam or complete a term paper. You have to sell yourself that the temporary pain right now (the all-nighters, the stress, the exhaustion, etc.) is worth the long-term gains (earning your degree, living a better life, etc.). Everything in life is a sale.

- **Having a positive mindset no matter what:** Everyone faces hardships, problems, and pain in life.

The ones who can sell themselves to stay positive no matter what will succeed. While the ones who sell themselves on playing the victim game end up failing.

We all know that playing the victim will get you nowhere in life. But when setbacks happen and obstacles come up, we have to sell ourselves to stay positive and take extreme ownership of everything good and bad in our lives.

If something bad happens to you, you can live a life in negativity like you are a victim and there is no hope. Or you can sell yourself to rise up, take extreme ownership, learn from the hardship, and push forward.

Selling yourself to view everything good or bad that happens to you as a learning lesson is a sale. Those who can stay positive win and those who stay negative lose.

- **Working out & eating healthy:** Forcing yourself to go to the gym and get a good workout in is a sale. Every day you have to sell yourself to get up, go to the gym, and push yourself physically. Every day you have to sell yourself to go harder with the cardio, the weights, etc. than you did the day before. Working out consistently is a sale that you have to close yourself on.

For most of us, it's really hard to eat healthy because junk food like burgers, candy, pizza, beer – all of that is so f*cking good. However, if you are serious about eating healthy and becoming the best you can be, you have to sell yourself that the short-term happiness of junk food won't be better than the long-term gains of eating healthy (losing weight, feeling better, etc.).

Your health is a sale, and every day you have a choice to either sell yourself to eat clean or sell yourself to eat badly.

Everything you eat is a sale.

- **Being happy is a sale:** You get to sell yourself and decide every day whether you are going to be happy or miserable. Happiness is a choice that requires you to sell yourself every day that life is a miracle. Just waking up breathing today is a gift and you should be ecstatic that you are even alive.

Not to get too deep on you but there are over an estimated 183,671 deaths per day. That's over 7,653 deaths per hour and 128 deaths per minute which equates to 2 deaths per second. All of these people would do anything to be alive vs the latter.

This stat on the daily death rate made me quickly realize and appreciate that just waking up every day is happiness. Anytime you start to get depressed, down, sad, stuck, etc.... Don't forget that just being alive is a gift and time on this earth is precious so choose to be happy over anything else.

- **Getting rid of toxic negative people in your life:** To get rid of the toxic people in your life you have to convince yourself that your network is your net worth.

You have to surround yourself with people who lift you up and help take you to the next level, not tear you down. You must sell yourself that removing these negative people as quickly as possible is required for success.

This sale can be difficult because getting rid of people you've had relationships with can hurt, but the quicker you level up your network, the quicker you soar to new heights.

- **Winning friends & influencing people:** To win new friends, keep old friends, and influence your friends to do what you want to do, you need to sell.

For example, let's say you meet someone with similar interests and hobbies. You need to sell them to exchange contact information and then you need to sell them again at that time or in the future to get together sometime.

Additionally, you need to sell your friends to invest their time, energy, and attention to keep developing the relationship. Even friendship is a sale and you have to work hard at selling your friends that you are valuable to them and they are valuable to you. This is why sales is required for all success. The faster you master sales the faster you get everything you want in life.

I hope you are now sold on the fundamental truth that sales is crucial to carving out the life you've always wanted.

SALES IS NECESSARY FOR SUCCESS

If you thought only salespeople have mastered selling, you totally thought wrong.

Sales is a life skill that all of the most successful people in the world have mastered.

Look at anyone in this world who's a top performer in their industry and you will see a common trend:

They're experts at selling others on their ideas, thoughts, vision, opinions, and mission.

They sold others on their ideas and closed sales with people to support them to make their dreams a reality.

All the success in the world exists because someone was good at sales and able to get others to support their ideas.

The ability to sell others and get them to believe in you is one of the top secrets to success.

When you know how to sell to get what you want in life, this is when you can truly serve others and make a positive impact.

No matter who you are, what you do, where you come from, what your background is, or whether you have a college degree or not… you're either making sales or losing sales.

The faster you understand and embody this success principle, the faster you will maximize your success in business, relationships, and life.

If you are a great salesperson. If you have the critical thinking skills and the communication skills to push the odds in your favor in every situation in life, you will be able to achieve your greatest success and your greatest potential.

If you don't want to leave your career, your success, and your life in the hands of "luck," "hope," and "wishful thinking," you have to learn how to persuade, how to influence, and how to sell.

WHY YOU SHOULD GET A JOB IN TECH SALES

Now that you know why mastering sales is the #1 secret to your success… I want to share the top reasons why tech sales is the greatest job in the world, and why you made a great decision to pick up a copy of *The Ultimate Guide To Breaking Into Tech Sales*.

THE AHA MOMENT:
FROM JANITOR TO TECH SALES MILLIONAIRE

The moment I realized sales was the greatest job in the world was when I went from working as a janitor, working like a dog from 5 AM to 3 PM for $6.00 / hour, to working at a call center where I made my first sale.

At the time when I was working as a janitor, my life was truly terrible, and that isn't an exaggeration.

I hated waking up. I hated going to work and I wanted to quit it all. Getting up every day to scrape gum off of 500 desks and clean up after kids, only for them to get everything dirty all over again was misery.

I finally mustered up the courage to quit that shitty job when I saw an ad for a technology call center with "unlimited commissions."

The starting pay was $7.50 (which doesn't sound like a lot now but trust me, for the time this was pretty good money). And for every $100 I sold over the phone, I got another $0.25 raise per hour for that pay period.

My big AHA moment (when I realized how lucrative sales is) happened on my first day at the call center. That day, I made my first sale over the phone to a complete stranger, and I got paid for my results vs. the hours I had to put in at the janitor gig to earn the same amount of money.

Do you want to know the crazy part too?

At the call center, I technically didn't have an actual product to sell.

I was cold calling people and asking for hundreds of dollars in donations for local police departments, firefighter unions, and other not-for-profit agencies in exchange for a sticker or a tax write-off.

Do you know how hard it is to cold call someone and ask them for a donation in exchange for no physical product other than a sticker to put on their car or a thank you receipt from their local firefighting department? It's incredibly hard!! Nearly impossible!

A product that eliminates a customer's pains, helps them solve their biggest problems, or achieve their greatest dreams is much easier to sell.

Nonetheless, on my first day, after making countless calls, I was able to sell a few hundred dollars and help a lot of organizations in the process.

With that first paycheck, I tripled my hourly rate in commissions even though I only worked 1/4th of the hours I clocked in at my janitor job.

That's when it hit me...

I can sit in an office making calls, selling people on products that can help change the world, and get paid for the results I drive, instead of getting paid for time exchanged and hours worked.

With this call center job, at first, I was just happy that I didn't have to wake up at 4 AM and clean a school all day. But when I discovered the potential for financial freedom with sales, it dawned on me that I could make bigger, transformative changes to my life.

On top of the flexible hours, I could make more money than I ever dreamed of (while still in high school at this time) working at this call center and selling donations for non-profit organizations.

Plus, if I decided to give it my all and make a career for myself in sales, I could spare myself from ever having to work hard manual labor ever again.

This is when I first truly learned that tech sales is the greatest job in the world if you go all in to master the job.

TECH SALES IS THE ULTIMATE TRIFECTA

I love tech sales and you should too because it's REPEATABLE, PREDICTABLE, & SCALABLE.

I call this the ultimate trifecta.

Albert Einstein once said, "Compounding interest is the eighth wonder of the world. He who understands it earns it; he who doesn't, pays it."

I love this quote. But I believe that the 8th wonder of the world is actually tech sales and here's why...

After working at the call center throughout high school, it was time to prep for college.

I knew going into college I had to get out of cold calling for donations and get into selling something tech-related because the internet and web technologies were taking the world by storm.

Tech was growing faster than any other industry out there, and I knew I had to be a part of it.

That's when during my first quarter of my freshman year, I got into tech sales and launched my own company for a lifelong passion of mine, online gambling.

After running this company for three years, building lists, prospecting, setting appointments, and selling, I generated over $12,000,000 in sales and became financially free.

$12,000,000 sounds impressive, but with this company, I found out firsthand that tech sales was the future because everything is so repeatable, predictable, and scalable. In fact, it's actually easy to generate $12,000,000 fast when you factor this in.

If you can close 1 sale in tech, you can quickly close 10 sales. If you can close 10 sales in tech, you can quickly close 100 sales. If you can close 100, you can easily multiply it and close 1,000.

Let's say you make $100,000 in tech sales. If you put in the hard work, dedication, and motivation. And if you have the technologies I share with you as well as the training... you can easily make $1,000,000,000 in tech sales like I did.

Tech sales is the only job that is highly repeatable, predictable, and scalable to millions.

If you want to go from broke to financially free, then getting a job and mastering tech sales is the answer!

HOW I USED TECH SALES TO BUILD A $1,000,000,000 COMPANY

Throughout my career, I started multiple tech companies and sold for multiple tech companies.

Some of my startups were successful, and many were massive failures. That being said, whenever I was down, I could always turn to tech sales to get back up on my feet and quickly go from broke to financially free while doing fulfilling work that changes people's lives for the better.

During college, I built a mobile marketing software called EnMobile that lost me millions of dollars and four years of my life because I relied on marketing instead of sales.

When this massive failure happened, I walked away from entre-preneurship, dusted myself off, and returned to sales, working as a business-to-business (B2B) tech salesperson for IBM and Google.

Not only did I eventually dig myself out of the debt hole and become a millionaire, but these tech sales jobs led me to my $100,000,000 idea with Seamless.AI.

You see, during my time at IBM and Google, I found that I wasted 50% of my days on non-selling activities like list-building, CRM data entry, and scouring millions of websites looking for people's emails and phone numbers.

All this mind-numbing, non-selling work was killing my potential because I could have been using that time to work on pitching and closing new sales.

I knew I had to figure out a way to automate all those tasks, so I could spend more time doing what I do best… closing tech sales.

So with an amazing team of engineers, we built a search engine powered by artificial intelligence that does all the hard work for you, and we called this search engine, Seamless.AI. Seamless finds all the contacts and companies in the world you need to sell to, and then uses artificial intelligence to research their perfect cell phones, emails, and direct dials in seconds.

The platform was such a success that the founder of Google and his wife invested in it, as well as Amazon, Guy Kawasaki (Head of Apple Products), and many others.

By automating the majority of my tech sales work, I quickly went from making six figures a year in sales, to making six figures a month in tech sales…

You read that right… With my secret software, I went from taking a year to make $100,000, to doing it every single month with predictability down to the dollar and the day.

This is what I mean when I say that tech sales is repeatable, predictable, and scalable. No other job can come close to beating it.

With all the money I was making, I eventually quit my tech sales jobs and turned Seamless into a full-fledged company where I could help tech salespeople across the globe accomplish the same results I had when I was using Seamless at my Google and IBM jobs.

We even launched a famous award for our 300,000+ salespeople who use the product every day called the President's Club Award.

When you make over $100,000 in sales, you win our famous SIX FIGURE CLUB AWARD.

And when you make over $1,000,000 in sales, you win our famous SEVEN FIGURE CLUB AWARD.

Hundreds of people win these awards every month and you can check out their stories here at:

www.PresidentsClubAwards.com

Within a few years of launching Seamless.AI, the salespeople that use the platform every day have booked over 13 million appointments, closed over 7 million sales, generated over $28 Billion in revenue, and now the company is valued at over $500,000,000 - $1,000,000,000.

I don't share this story to brag, but to show you that tech sales can change your life forever.

Companies like Seamless only demonstrate the fact that you can get a job in this profession, and build generational wealth faster than any other career.

WHY TECH SALES IS
THE BEST JOB IN THE WORLD

Before I teach you how to get a job in tech sales and make $100,000 a year, I want to help you avoid the top reason why salespeople fail in tech.

Can you guess what it is?

It's not confidence or lack thereof. It's not poor cold-call scripts. It's not years of experience. It's not bad sales technology (Could be if you aren't using Seamless.AI). It's not poor tonality. And it's not a lack of hard work...

The top reason people fail at tech sales is because they aren't sold on going all in with this profession.

As they prospect for tech sales jobs, they keep thinking, *There must be something better out there that I could be doing than this.*

And when they finally get the job and start working, they get slammed with the inevitable hard work, and mentally return to that belief that there's something better out there... and they quit.

Anything that creates financial freedom is hard at first. But if you keep going and never give up you will achieve massive success.

I promise you that. I just need you to go all in with me and believe it.

Don't let that voice in your head tell you to quit when it gets hard applying for jobs or when you face your first challenge at work to turn strangers into buying customers.

I want to help you avoid making the mistake millions of people make in tech sales by quitting as soon as things get a little hard because this profession changed the trajectory of my life, and I know it will change yours.

My goal is to be your coach and to teach you everything you need to know to flood your calendar with back-to-back job interviews and help you land that dream sales job.

I am here for you as your friend and partner throughout your journey in tech sales. However, I cannot have you ever think about quitting along the way.

I want to remove any doubts you may have about this career and help you realize that technology sales will make all of your goals and dreams come true.

It's so important that I sell you on tech sales because once you're sold, you can own your job hunt 100%.

And when you get your new tech sales job, you can bring all the energy to crush it and become a top performer.

But first, to get you sold on tech sales, I want to highlight some of the top reasons why this is the greatest job in the world:

You can make more than everyone you know:

Tech salespeople are some of the highest earners in the professional world. You can easily out-earn doctors, lawyers, and accountants without spending years in college racking up student loan debt.

You can work from anywhere:

You can sell from anywhere in tech sales. Your house, a Starbucks, an Airbnb on the ocean, you name it. The ability to work remotely is such a luxury, especially in these times. You can literally make sales happen whenever and wherever you are, as long as you have an internet connection! Having the ability to work remotely gives you the ultimate freedom to move where you want.

You get to positively impact other people's lives:

Sales allows you to enhance someone's life, their business, and their success by introducing them to a solution that will solve their biggest problems and help them achieve their greatest dreams. There's honestly no greater feeling.

No college degree required:

One of the greatest perks of building a career in sales is that you don't need a college degree.

College teaches you very little about sales. So often, most of your sales education is going to come from sales books like this one or sales training. Those resources will teach you more about communication and sales than you could learn in college.

Additionally, tech sales is one of the few professions where you can generate six or seven figures without a degree. I have friends who never went to college and are making $100,000 to $1,500,000 in sales. With sales you don't have to rack up $100,000 in debt for a degree you never end up using.

You get rewarded by a meritocracy vs. political bureaucracy:

Sales is a meritocracy, which means the harder you work and the more results you generate, the more you get paid.

With other jobs it doesn't matter how hard you work, you're going to be stuck at the same salary rate for a while before you ever get a raise.

In sales, the commissions and promotions you earn are based solely on the results you generate, not who you know, who you suck up to, or any kind of politics you play. Your success is completely yours for the making.

If every day you hit every channel (call, email, social media, etc.), read sales books, prospect, and practice the scripts and the playbooks, you will eventually become a top earner and get rewarded. Period.

Tech sales is repeatable, scalable, and predictable:

Once you figure out how to prospect, pitch, and close new customers in tech, you can easily scale or multiply the results you drive with more work.

This means if you can sell a tech product to 10 people, then you can easily figure out how to sell it to 100 people. If you can sell a tech product to 100 people, then you can easily figure out how to sell it to 1,000 people. If you can sell a tech product to 1,000 people, then you can figure out how to sell it to 10,000 people and easily scale that up to millions of customers like the top tech companies.

And as soon as you figure out the right sales systems and the right sales processes for the product or service you sell, you can scale the sales you generate.

So if you can generate $10,000 in sales, you can easily figure out how to generate $100,000 in sales… And once you generate $100,000 in sales, you can easily figure out how to generate $1,000,000 in sales.

Selling for tech companies is the fastest way to achieve life-changing wealth.

You get to become an intrepreneur vs. losing it all as an entrepreneur:

When you work in sales, you get to become an intrepreneur at your own company. Instead of risking all your money and not making anything for years as an "entrepreneur," you earn a salary plus commission and you get to build your own book of business (your personal list of clients). If you ever wanted to become an entrepreneur, tech sales is the best way to do it without all the risk. You get to network, market, pitch an innovative product, and grow your own clientele, as an intrepreneur!

You get 100% control:

Unlike other careers, where your promotion and the money you make are determined by someone else, in sales you have total control over the success of your career and the path you take.

You never have to worry about finding a job:

Tech salespeople are always in high demand. Companies can't hire enough sales reps because the more reps your team has, the better your odds are of driving more revenue. Additionally, because salespeople are in such high demand, salary offers are at an all-time high. Now is a great time to get into sales. And there are no signs that this trend is ending soon.

It's easy to get into tech sales:

Most sales jobs have a low barrier to entry, which means they don't require special training or certification to get started. This makes sales one of the most accessible jobs for people beginning their professional careers. Having a commitment to helping your customers and an energetic passion for sales can often be enough to help you get an entry-level sales job that turns into a lucrative, lifelong career helping others.

Investors love tech companies and tech salespeople:

On average, investors give out the largest valuations (10x to 30x) per $1 made in sales at tech companies. So if a tech company's sales team generates $1 in sales, an investor will value that business anywhere from $10 to $30. If you work in tech sales for a tech company doing $10,000,000... it's probably worth at least $100,000,000 to investors.

The main reason investors place so much value on tech companies is because they know these organizations can grow easily and scale faster than any other industry.

If investors are giving the highest return on investment in valuations to technology companies because of their growth potential, this also means that *selling* for technology companies offers the greatest growth potential for you and your career.

Tech products are the most repeatable, predictable, and scalable to sell, and that's why investors love them. You should love it too!

You get the ultimate freedom:

Few jobs provide the freedom that salespeople enjoy. Sure, sales objectives are set by leadership at the organization, but sales reps determine how they reach those goals, how they spend their time, and the activities they do to drive results.

You learn the soft skills that employers are looking for:

Recruiters love candidates with soft skills (i.e. great communication skills, ability to work well with others, etc.) because these are skills you can't teach. Sales challenges you to perfect soft skills like communication, problem-solving, negotiation, and teamwork. This means you will be a top candidate in the job market.

Tech sales gives you work-life balance:

Every salesperson is given a quota for the year. It doesn't matter how early or late in the year you do it, but as soon as you crush that quota you can take time off and do what you want to do or you can work more and any more sales commission you rake in will just be extra play money.

You learn the tech skills that employers value the most:

By learning the ins and outs of the tech product you sell, you learn important skills and gain a ton of tech experience, which is always in high demand.

You get to rub shoulders with BOSSES:

You get to put yourself in front of decision-makers, leaders, and department heads and introduce them to the latest & greatest tech. 'Nuff said!

You feed the success of every department at your company (total bragging rights):

Many tech companies look to their sales talent pool when they need to fill positions in their marketing and customer success departments because it's less costly to hire internally than to recruit outside candidates. As a result, sales can always be an entry point into careers in marketing or customer success.

You experience unlimited personal and professional growth:

With all the training, practice, and improvement you have to make every day, sales will whip you into shape and turn you into the best version of yourself.

What's even better is that most companies will pay for sales team training, so you're often improving on your company's dollar.

Thriving in sales can be hard work, but hard is good. There's something to be said about going to a job where you are challenged to become the best you can be every single day.

Sales works for any personality:

It doesn't matter if you're an introvert or an extrovert, if you learn the key sales strategy, secrets, and principles, you can sell anyone on anything that you need to. It doesn't matter whether you're shy and reserved or loud and outgoing, sales allows you to stay true to who you are and make this profession your own.

You can get promoted quickly:

Entry-level sales reps can get promoted to higher titles like "Account Executive" and even managerial positions FAST. You just have to work hard and consistently drive results.

Your network becomes your net worth:

With tech sales, you get to work with new people every day. And as you build new connections and generate more sales, your network and your net worth grow.

You learn how to sell people on your ideas, your talents, and your abilities:

Whether you're interviewing for a job, asking for a salary raise, or a promotion, sales will help you advocate for yourself and get what you want.

You get to join a highly motivated community:

The team atmosphere of sales allows you to share all types of experiences. You work in the trenches together, you win together, you lose together, you bring each other up, you hit the gong to celebrate new sales together, and you learn in the process. There isn't a more inspiring team of people to work with than a sales team.

You get to travel the world:

Whether you're hitting the airport for conferences, huge deal opportunities, networking opportunities, or new market research – sales allows you to travel the world.

Tech sales is fun:

When you have an amazing product and you're great at what you do, sales will feel less like a job and more like a fun game where you get to compete with your teammates for the top sales spot every month, and celebrate each other's wins.

You learn a necessary life skill:

Because everything in life is a sale (from school to your job to personal relationships) if you hone your sales skills, you're set for life.

You get to educate people on the latest trends and greatest products:

As a salesperson, you get to play "teacher" to your prospects. You get to educate them on how they can increase their efficiency, increase their productivity, solve their problems, and make their lives easier.

You get to positively impact the world:

It's literally your job to make a positive impact in the world. You get to make people's lives easier! Oh, and the more people you positively impact, the more money you make! What other job in the world does that?

Every day is an adventure:

No two days are alike in sales. Every day will present new opportunities and challenges that make the job exciting. Plus you'll constantly meet new people from different industries. Tech sales may be a lot of things, but boring isn't one of them!

You are one of the most important people at any company:

From new projects to new programs and policies, sales is the fuel that brings in the money to make everything else possible at any business. If the economy crashes, as a salesperson, you will be the last person to get fired. Sales is the ultimate job security.

Winning new sales boosts your confidence and is the greatest feeling in the world:

Winning new sales will give you one of the greatest feelings in the world. It will also boost your overall confidence and only make you better at your job. When you generate six, seven, or eight figures in sales, you get the ultimate bragging rights of being a top earner at your company as well!

You learn how to become unstoppable in good times and bad:

Sales teaches you lifelong lessons because you have to perform during good economic times and bad economic times. To succeed in bad economies, sales teaches you tenacity and how to tough it out when things get hard, which is one of the most important skills you will ever need in life.

You're forced to constantly level up your game:

At every company, the sales must grow month to month. There's no room for complacency. This pushes you to step things up every day and to not only elevate your game but elevate the results you generate.

You get to interact with a wide range of people:

If you're a people person, if you love meeting new people and you're a great conversationalist, sales is the career where you get to express that passion for people.

You get to make an immediate impact at your job:

As a salesperson, you bring in the revenue that makes it possible for every department to thrive, from contributing funds to salaries and budgets. This means that you play an integral part at a company as soon as you start. There's no waiting around for things to heat up and having to do a bunch of busy work.

You get to build lifelong relationships:

It's hard to think of a profession where personal connections are more foundational than sales. As sales professionals, we have the privilege of cultivating meaningful relationships with our customers. From the people you prospect to your new customers and the network you build, you get paid to build new relationships.

Tech sales is fulfilling and helps you become the best you can be:

A career in tech sales is stimulating and fulfilling. You get to work with intelligent people who are at the top of their game, solve meaningful challenges, and develop skills that can be useful for a lifetime. You get better and smarter every day. You subconsciously improve at your job with every interaction. The more experience you have in sales, the stronger your sales skills become.

Tech sales will set you free:

I hope with my story you can see for yourself that not only is sales the greatest profession in the world, but tech sales is the greatest job in the world.

If you can learn how to sell in tech, you can do anything.

Tech sales radically changed my life, and it will change your life too!

I went from being a janitor, earning $6.00 an hour, to getting into tech sales. And within tech sales, I went from generating $100,000 a year to $100,000 a month to now making hundreds of thousands a day! The amazing profession of tech sales helped my team and I grow our company from $0 to now being worth over $1 Billion in just a few years.

I am writing this book because I want you to go all in on becoming the best you can be in technology sales so you can change your life forever.

I want to help you get a job in tech sales because the life you want, the family you want, the freedom you want, and the money you want are going to be fueled by a tech sales career.

I am living, breathing proof that mastering tech sales can change your life forever for the better. There are thousands of other people who started out just like you and are now ultra successful from tech sales too.

Getting a job in tech sales will be one of the most rewarding decisions of your life.

I hope I helped you eliminate any doubts or concerns you have about getting a job in tech sales. And I hope this has inspired you to go all in on the #1 job in the world. Let's go make it happen!

MYTHS ABOUT WORKING IN SALES

For most of my life, sales has always been a job that a lot of people looked down on.

Growing up, my teachers, counselors, and friends would tell me that if I wanted to become successful, I had to become a doctor, a lawyer, or an accountant.

And on the flip side, if you started work in sales, the assumption was that you had no talent, no intelligence, and no work ethic.

Myths like this are the reason why I wrote this book. I want to help save you from this inaccurate advice because what the world doesn't tell you is that the most successful billionaires and millionaires are all salespeople.

What all the mentors in your life, from your professors to your parents, don't teach you is that sales is the highest-paying job you can get.

If you become great at sales you will make 3x, 5x, or even 10x more than your lawyer, doctor, stock trader, or accountant friends guaranteed.

The salespeople I know in my network are filthy rich. They are millionaires, multi-millionaires, and even billionaires, making $250,000 - $10,000,000+ a year depending on the products they sell.

And my network isn't the exception either...

Because I don't want you to ever have doubts or questions about building your successful sales career, I came up with a list of the top sales myths out there, and how to overcome them.

MYTH: I NEED TO HAVE SALES EXPERIENCE

Truth: You do not need to have any experience to be successful at your first sales job. Never forget that anyone you see who is wildly successful in sales today started with zero experience at one point. Nonetheless, they didn't let this stop them. They learned on the job and during their time off. They read, they studied, they practiced, and now they are unstoppable.

MYTH: I NEED TO BE SMART

Truth: You do not need to be a tech genius to thrive in sales. I was a C student throughout school. None of my teachers thought I would amount to anything. But despite what they thought of my potential, I still created huge success for myself in sales.

To crush it in sales, you don't need exceptional intelligence. In fact, I've seen many Ivy League graduates fail at sales because they tended to overthink everything. They always ended up quitting. If you want to be a top performer, you just need to be positive, coachable, hardworking, and willing to do whatever it takes to get the job done!

MYTH: SALESPEOPLE ARE SCAM ARTISTS SELLING THINGS PEOPLE DON'T WANT OR NEED

Truth: Some people look negatively at sales because there are a select few who have given the profession a bad name.

You've got box office smash hits making criminal salespeople famous, and occasionally you see news stories about con artist salespeople selling something to people that they don't want or need.

This isn't sales. This is fraud. Don't let these types of people fool you. These people are not noble. They are criminals.

Sales isn't the only profession where a select few people do dumb criminal acts. You will find scam artists in every field, including medicine, law, education, business, and politics.

My advice to you is to never let the one criminal out of the tens of millions of salespeople hold you back from getting into this industry.

MYTH: I NEED TO BE A SMOOTH TALKER

Truth: Salespeople have a reputation for being smooth talkers. But with all my experience in this industry, I honestly don't even really know what a smooth talker is! You don't need to be an eloquent speaker with a silver tongue to do well in tech sales. You just need to genuinely care about the customer, and be passionate about removing their pains to get their goals fulfilled. If you have a sincere passion for your customers, knowing exactly what to say will naturally follow.

MYTH: I NEED TO BE CONFIDENT

Truth: Most salespeople aren't confident. Believe it or not, there are more introverts in sales than extroverts. So if you aren't an outgoing person, this isn't a big deal. The quality you need to work on is your fearlessness.

When you get a sales job, you will represent a company and a product that can change someone's life for the better. This will require you to believe in yourself 100%.

When you have conviction in yourself, your product, and the positive impact it will have on others, your confidence will shine through without any effort on your part.

MYTH: I NEED TO BE POPULAR AND HAVE A LOT OF CONNECTIONS TO BE SUCCESSFUL

Truth: Everyone starts with nothing in sales. So if you aren't coming in with lots of connections, don't worry because you aren't alone. As soon as you begin your job, make a point to prospect and build your book of business every single day on social media, at networking events, etc.

I've built a company worth $100 Million in 2.5 years and $1 Billion in 5 years. While this might sound impressive, I started with no connections and no network.

If I can do it, you can too. You just have to be diligent.

MYTH: I WILL BE ON THE PHONE ALL DAY

Truth: Luckily for you, this is not Wall Street in the 1980s where the only way to reach a prospect was on the phone. Sales today is all about leveraging a multi-channel sales campaign, which means using calls, email, LinkedIn, video, and text to connect with your customers. This is because the more activity you do, the more money you make. If this sounds complicated, don't worry! I will teach you how to run multi-channel sales campaigns in this book to achieve massive success.

MYTH: I HAVE TO USE SHADY TACTICS

Truth: This is a flat-out lie, and one of the reasons that sales gets a bad rep. Great salespeople don't use shady tactics and they sell with integrity. Their #1 priority is always doing right by their customers, their company, and their network. In sales, you can only be successful if you take a servant approach and work hard to help and serve your customers at the highest levels. When you take a servant's approach you will never need to use shady tactics.

MYTH: I WON'T MAKE ANY MONEY IN SALES

Truth: You will make more money than you ever dreamed of in sales. By learning and executing the secrets I teach you in this book, you will become financially free.

Don't believe me? Check out the proof:

At Seamless.AI, we've helped over 16,000 people make over $100,000 in sales.

We've helped over 5,000 people make over $1,000,000 in sales.

We've helped over 500 people make over $10,000,000 in sales. If they can do it, so can you!

My team and I need you to achieve success so we can see you on stage winning our famous President's Club Awards:

www.PresidentsClubAwards.com

MYTH: I WON'T BE HAPPY

Truth: Yes you will! You will love your job. You will make more money than you ever dreamed of. And you will accomplish all of your goals and dreams... Want to know why I know this? Because you will learn the playbooks, systems, processes, lists, scripts, training, mindset, and activity required to be successful.

The people who are miserable at sales don't invest in books like this. And as a result, it takes them longer to learn these lessons I'm going to share with you. The more you invest in learning everything in this book and taking the action to execute, the more money you will make.

MYTH: I WILL BE SUPER STRESSED ABOUT HITTING MY QUOTA EVERY MONTH

Truth: The only people who are constantly worried about quota are the ones who don't have a repeatable, scalable, and predictable sales system to generate results. This book teaches you all of that, so when you land your sales job, you'll be well ahead of your peers month after month.

MYTH: I WILL HAVE TO PRESSURE PEOPLE INTO BUYING

Truth: Despite popular belief, sales is not about pushing a product down someone's throat who doesn't need it or is not interested. That's not what great salespeople do. Great salespeople understand their customers' needs and they help them find the right solution to meet or exceed their goals. When you create a business case that shows the pros, the cons, and the ROI (return on investment) of your product or service, new customers will form a line out the door to buy! You will not have to pressure anyone into buying because I'm going to teach you how to find people who desperately need and want your services.

MYTH: SALES IS NOT A PRESTIGIOUS CAREER

Truth: Sales is the wealthiest occupation in the world. More importantly, sales is a servant profession, where every day you get up and connect with people who desperately need your products or services to improve the overall quality of their lives. There's nothing more honorable or prestigious than that.

Now that we've broken down some of the biggest misconceptions about sales, I hope you fully understand that sales is the greatest job in the world.

Now let's wrap up PART 1 so you can start prospecting for your dream tech sales job.

WHO THIS BOOK IS FOR

One of the greatest things about tech sales is that this profession is for anyone, regardless of education, background, or experience.

If you want to get into one of the most rewarding, exciting, and challenging careers in the world, then *The Ultimate Guide To Breaking Into Tech Sales* is the book for you.

Below is a list of the different types of people this book is perfect for, as well as some motivational reasons why you should go all in with building a successful career in tech sales:

- People who want to break out into one of the most lucrative industries in the world.

- People who want to go from broke to financially free as quickly as possible.

- College students and graduates who want to start a lifelong career where they can have complete ownership of their success.

- People who want to create the life they've always dreamed of.

- Anyone (with some sales experience or none), who wants to change jobs and make the jump to tech sales.

- People who want to make more money and have unlimited commissions.

- People who want to get paid for the actual work they put in. The more work you put into tech sales, the more money you can make. Period.

- People who want to transition from a slow-growing company to a fast-growing tech industry!

- People who are sick of being a victim of circumstances, tired of making excuses, and ready to take control of their life.

- People who are ready to put in the work and take the action to change their life forever and for the better. The people who take the most action generate the greatest success, results, and money.

THE GOAL OF THIS BOOK

It is my life's mission to help you connect to opportunity, make millions in sales, achieve financial freedom, and positively impact billions.

Throughout my career in tech sales, thousands of people have reached out to me, and a lot of them have asked the same question, "How do I get a job in tech sales like you?"

With this book, it's my mission to answer this question and help you accomplish two goals in life:

#1. I NEED YOU TO GET A JOB IN TECH SALES AND BECOME FINANCIALLY FREE!

Tech sales changed my life. I was able to wipe out my debt, travel the world, buy the houses and cars that I always wanted, and live a stress-free life.

I need you to get a job in tech sales so that you can do the same and create the dream life that you and your loved ones deserve.

You have unlimited potential, and the only way for me to help you capitalize on that potential is by helping you get a job in tech sales making over $100,000 / year.

#2. I NEED YOU TO WIN OUR FAMOUS PRESIDENT'S CLUB AWARD

I remember the first time I made over $100,000 in just one month.

Now my company and I make $100,000 - $500,000 every single day.

These events were all life-changing for my family, our company, our employees, our investors, and the 300,000+ sales teams who use Seamless.AI every day.

Every time I reached a big milestone, I couldn't believe it happened.

I didn't believe it was possible for someone like me, who came from a blue-collar family.

I never believed it was possible for a kid out of the east side of Cleveland who never did well in school and was always told he would never make it.

Even though I grew up in such poor circumstances, I never accepted these temporary conditions as my permanent reality. I did whatever it took to build a better life for myself.

I know if I can do it, you can too.

That is why I wrote this book, why we built Seamless.AI, and most importantly, why my team and I launched the President's Club Awards (**www.PresidentsClubAwards.com**)!

My goal for you over the next year is to get a job in tech sales and win our famous President's Club Awards featured in the picture below:

The President's Club Awards is a celebration of your sales success along this incredible journey to becoming the best that you can be in tech sales.

We want to be there with you every step of the way, celebrating all of your major sales achievements throughout your career.

So when you get your dream tech sales job and make **over $100,000 in sales**, I will send you a custom **Six Figure Club Award** to hang on your wall (the gold award pictured on the left).

What's even better is, when you **make over $1,000,000 in sales**, I will send you our most prized award to hang on your wall, **The Seven Figure Club Award** (the platinum award pictured on the right).

You can hang these awards on your wall or put them right above your computer, so when you are prospecting, pitching, and closing deals all day long, you can use them as motivation to keep selling, working hard, and doing whatever it takes to provide for you and your family.

I want you to win this award, just like I did, and thousands of other people have. I want your entire wall filled with these! When you generate six figures in sales, apply for your award at:

www.PresidentsClubAwards.com

You may be asking yourself, "Why is getting into the Seven Figure Club so important to Brandon?"

It's because I know the more money you make, the more people you can help positively impact!

Your goal, your dream, your vision, and all of your hard work this next year should be invested in getting a job in tech sales and winning our famous President's Club Award ASAP!

Let's work hard together to make this next year your biggest and best yet.

I know you can win this award. Let's make it happen together!

SEE IT, BELIEVE IT, ACHIEVE IT

I know it's hard to imagine making over $100,000 or $1,000,000 in sales.

I get it. I was just like you and I never believed it was possible for someone like me either…

Then I started hearing stories about all these successful tech salespeople making millions…

And none of them were exceptionally talented.

Many of them were just everyday people like you and me.

From then on whenever I had any doubts, I would think about those stories and remind myself, if they could achieve life-changing wealth for themselves, I could too.

That's why I am excited to share with you how many people have won our famous President's Club Awards.

They aren't smarter, better educated, wealthier, or more talented than you.

They just believed in going all in and doing whatever it takes at their tech sales job to make it happen.

When you see success, you can achieve success. So check out the results below of some of our President's Club winners, get your job in tech sales, help a lot of prospects solve their problems, make a ton of sales, and apply for your award at:

www.PresidentsClubAwards.com

- **Six Figure President's Club Winners:** We've helped over **16,000 salespeople** make **over $100,000 in sales** and win our famous Six Figure Club Award.

- **Seven Figure President's Club Winners:** We've helped over **5,000 salespeople** make over **$1,000,000 in sales** and win our famous Seven Figure Club Award.

- **Eight Figure President's Club Winners:** We've helped over **500 salespeople** make over **$10,000,000 in sales** and win our famous Eight Figure Club Award.

- **Seamless.AI Software Results:** People using our sales software, sales training, sales books, and sales secrets have booked over 13,843,138 appointments, closed over 2,768,628 deals, and generated over $27,686,275,480 in new revenue.

PART 1: WRAP-UP

We covered a lot here. By now you should be sold that the #1 secret to your success is to master sales.

You should believe with 100% certainty that sales is a skill required to maximize every aspect of life, and the key to all your successes.

In addition to this, you've learned why it's imperative to get a job in tech sales... Why the stereotypes out there about sales are all false limiting beliefs that people made up... As well as the ultimate goal of this book, which is to help you get your job in tech sales ASAP and start your journey to winning our famous President's Club Awards.

Now it's time to teach you the step-by-step system you need to get a job in tech sales. We'll teach you the marketing and self-promotion you need to launch, how to build your prospecting lists for new jobs, and the scripts and campaigns you'll have to create so you book tons of interviews and get job offers as quickly as possible.

Let's dive in to make this next year your biggest and best yet.

Part 2 is going to be FIRE!

PAY IT FORWARD

One of the best things you can do in life is give to others without expecting anything in return.

When you pay it forward and help others without expecting anything in return… Magical things happen!

You feel better about yourself and you create a ripple effect where the people you help go on to help others.

As you continue reading this book, if you think it helps you at all in your job search… Would you please consider writing an Amazon review right now?

The more reviews the book has, the easier it will be for others just like you to find this book and start reading it to transform their lives.

Plus, when you write an Amazon review, we will hook you up with 10 AMAZING Bonuses…

If you're wondering how much all these bonuses will cost you… It will only take 60 seconds of your time and I'm personally going to reward you with $1,935.97 in bonuses as a thank you.

You read that right!

Take 60 seconds out of your day to write a review, screenshot it, and upload it at **www.BrandonBornancin.com/techsalesbonus** and all ten bonuses are yours absolutely free!

You are just one review away from changing someone's life forever and for the better.

Thank you for paying it forward.

Write an Amazon Review Here: **www.amzn.to/3Yki4qT**

Write a Book Review & Get Over $1,935 in Bonuses!

Claim your FREE Bonus Bundle

EVERYTHING YOU'RE GOING TO GET:

- Unlock *Whatever It Takes* – The ultimate guide to building top sales habits, eliminating the bad ones, and maximizing your success in tech sales, relationships, and life! (Value $29.97)

- Get **Seamless.AI** – The #1 sales software to find cell phones, emails, and direct dials for anyone using artificial intelligence. Over $250 Credits Free! (Value $250)

- Get your very own **Tech Sales Earnings Calculator** – The only tool you need to easily calculate your path to earning $100K in tech sales FAST! (Value $147)

- Get **The Big 150 HR List** HR People Don't Want You To Have! This list includes 150+ Titles for every HR and recruiting title you need to prospect so you book more interviews and get in… (Value $257)

- Crush your goals, book more interviews than ever before and sign that dream job offer sooner than later with the help of our behind the scenes **Sales Activity Tracker!** (Value $147)

- Full access to the **Sales Secrets Master Class** – Over 100+ hours of exclusive interviews where the world's top sales experts reveal their secrets to success (Value $597)

- Get **Contact & Company Intelligence** – 50+ data points to personalize your outreach to recruiters and hiring managers, cut through the noise, and flood your calendar with job interviews (Value $207)

- Unlock the **Special Scripts Bonus** that includes 20 extra plug-and-play scripts you can use to connect with recruiters and hiring managers for every channel (from email to social) (Value $97)

- Immediate access to the **Job Offer Scoring Checklist** – A foolproof scoresheet to evaluate and compare your offers so you choose the job that's the perfect fit for you! (Value $107)

- Instant access to **The Top Secret Interview Questions**. Over 20+ of the most common tech sales interview questions that no one tells you to prepare for. Learn how to answer these to stack up the job offers!!! (Value $97)

Scan to Write a Review & Claim Bonuses!

Total Value: $1,935

www.BrandonBornancin.com/techsalesbonus

PART 2

THE MINDSET

T o be successful in tech sales, you need to have the right mindset for success.

To make over $100,000 in sales, you need to embody the mindset of doing "Whatever It Takes" (W.I.T.) to be successful.

With the right habits, mindset, and W.I.T. principles, you can accomplish anything.

More importantly, when we consider prospecting for jobs, having a Whatever It Takes mindset is the quality that will set you apart from the rest.

Most technology and SaaS companies are constantly looking for salespeople who embody these core values because they know these qualities will make the difference between success and failure.

Having the right mindset is so important to achieve success in business, relationships, and life. I even wrote a bestselling book on it called *Whatever It Takes: Master The Habits To Transform Your Business, Relationships, and Life!*

Listed below are the top operating principles or traits all recruiters look for when hiring entry-level and mid-level salespeople. These operating principles are the traits that all recruiters also look for in entry-level and mid-level salespeople to hire.

Your life will change forever for the better if you study these habits and represent them daily throughout your business and personal life.

POSITIVITY

Always have a positive mindset. Become bulletproof to negativity and don't let anyone hold you back.

It's important to realize that in life, you have two choices... You can either be a positive momentum builder, or a negative momentum killer.

Instead of being negative and dreading the inevitable challenges that will come up, bring a positive, "Can Do" attitude to every situation you encounter.

Have zero tolerance for negativity, and only embrace the "glass half-full" approach to every task and challenge.

COACHABILITY

Be humble, hungry, and the hardest working person in the room. Accept the fact that you don't know everything no matter how much experience or education you have. You can always learn something new to do it better, smarter, or faster.

Be open to learning from others on your team. I'm obsessed with getting better by 1% a day because by the end of the year all that minor yet consistent progress adds up to a 37x improvement from where I started. Be coachable and get better every day.

STRONG WORK ETHIC

Be the first person in, and the last person out. Stay hungry to achieve and put in the extra work to crush your goals – not for the shout-outs or the money – but for the sake of excellence.

INTELLIGENCE

Smart people who can't apply their knowledge during a real-life crisis tend to work slower than others because they overcomplicate things. You want to possess book smarts, but also have the common sense to know how to apply it.

INITIATIVE

Don't wait around for your manager or boss to walk you through your tasks. Instead, be proactive and take charge of your work.

INTEGRITY

If a company hires a rockstar with amazing talent but no sense of right and wrong, their reputation is on the line every day. Always do what's right legally, ethically, and professionally.

SOCIAL PROOF

You want to show a recruiter that they won't be taking a risk hiring you. Present a history of success with references (past employers, teachers, advisors, etc.).

Also, include any relevant work experience. Even if you've never worked in tech sales, you've probably developed plenty of skills for the job like communication and problem-solving (yes, even your experience at that mall job is fair game!).

Here at Seamless.AI, we've hired over 1,000 people, and most of these positions have been entry-level or mid-level sales positions.

In addition to the previous list, here are the core values our recruiters at Seamless look for in new hires:

WHATEVER IT TAKES MENTALITY

Be ready and willing to go all out for your customers, your company, and your goals.

THINK BIGGER

Think bigger than that new car or that expensive trip to Cancun. Have a mission that's bigger than yourself and makes a positive impact on the tech sales industry.

WHOLE > SELF

A team that works together can put out 5x what one rockstar employee can produce. Be a team player and show that you can put your team ahead of your own interests.

RESILIENCE

Be resilient and possess that tough grittiness that the world's top athletes have. Demonstrate the determination to endure even when you're facing failure.

OWNERSHIP

Own 100% of your goals and take full responsibility when you make mistakes.

NEVER FAIL

Failure is inevitable for everyone. But when you choose to learn from your failures instead of giving up, you really haven't failed, you've just grown and become better. Turn your failures into growth opportunities and learning lessons.

DO MORE WITH LESS

Learn how to do more with less. Be able to accomplish more with less money, less time, and less resources than originally expected. If you can take $1 and turn it into $10 vs. taking $1 and turning it into $2, you will always outperform the competition and become your manager's favorite person.

EMBRACE CHANGE

Tech sales changes every day. Be adaptable and willing to adjust to this change.

CHALLENGE EVERYTHING

When you're on the job, do you play by the book or do you look for ways things could be better? If you want a dream tech sales job, don't be the type to stick to the status quo until it becomes irrelevant. Follow the rules until you can find a better way of doing things. Ask yourself every day, "How can I do X better?"

These are all the skills and qualities you want to showcase in your resume (through your experience and references), your interview, and (honestly) all facets of your life.

The quicker you can embrace these qualities, the more success you will achieve.

Make it a point to actively work on these qualities every single day.

Additionally, think about examples, stories, and experiences from your personal and professional life where you exuded these qualities, and be ready to mention them so you can have an amazing interview and score that tech sales job!

REJECTION IS REQUIRED FOR SUCCESS

The best salespeople in the world are great at overcoming rejection and continuing to move forward to accomplish their goals no matter what. They don't let setbacks, rejection, or failure ever stop them or slow them down from achieving success.

They know that no matter how big and successful they get, they will still get rejected over and over again as they pursue bigger goals. Nonetheless, they make a promise to themselves and the companies they work for to never give up.

Top salespeople understand that failure is inevitable, however quitting is never an option.

If you want to be a top performer in tech sales, your only option is to fail forward and not only learn from your mistakes but use the lessons to strengthen your game plan for the future.

Bouncing back and failing forward is ultimately what separates the winners from the losers in sales.

I want you right now to promise me that you are going to go all in on getting a job in tech sales and doing whatever it takes to become the best salesperson that you can be, despite all the rejection you will face.

The people that give it their all and get back up every time they get knocked down are the people that change the world. The most successful people in the world are the ones who never give up no matter what.

I want to share some amazing stories about salespeople, entrepreneurs, inventors, athletes, celebrities and other ultra successful people who were faced with failure or told they would never be successful.

Against all odds, these people never gave up. And because of their tenacity, they have achieved massive success. Some of them have even become household names.

Use these stories to inspire you and motivate you to create the unstoppable tenacity you need to become the best salesperson:

If they can do it, you can too.

I hope these stories inspire you to persist no matter what failures you experience or obstacles life throws your way.

Instead of quickly moving on from rejection and learning nothing, embrace rejection because it's a necessary part of your journey to success in tech sales.

Michael Jordan: In high school, Michael Jordan was cut from the Varsity basketball team because he needed to "develop more." He's now considered the greatest basketball player of all time, with six NBA championships to his name and billions of dollars in endorsements. Michael Jordan's net worth is $1.7 Billion.

Elon Musk: Early in his career, when he was applying for internet jobs, Elon Musk was rejected by several companies. Musk would eventually transform the tech and luxury industries with the launch of Tesla and SpaceX. Despite Tesla and SpaceX nearly going bankrupt, the two companies are thriving and today Elon Musk is worth $265 Billion.

Albert Einstein: Albert Einstein didn't speak a complete sentence until he was five years old. Despite his presumably "slow-paced development," Einstein would eventually become a certified genius and a Nobel Prize-winning physicist, developing the theory of relativity.

J.K. Rowling: J.K. Rowling was a single mother on welfare when she wrote the first Harry Potter book, and this manuscript was rejected by 12 different publishers. Now, with 500 million copies sold worldwide, the Harry Potter book series is the bestselling book series of all time. J.K. Rowling's net worth is approximately $1 Billion.

Thomas Edison: It took Thomas Edison 10,000 attempts to finally perfect the first electric light bulb. Because Edison refused to give up, he created one of the most essential inventions in the modern era. With over 1,000 patents, Edison is the most prolific inventor in U.S. history.

Oprah Winfrey: Oprah Winfrey was fired from her first TV anchor job. She went on to become the host of the highest-rated talk show in television history (*The Oprah Winfrey Show*), the founder and owner of her own production company (Harpo Productions), and the first black female billionaire. Oprah Winfrey's net worth is $2.5 Billion.

Walt Disney: At his first job as a newspaper cartoonist, Walt Disney was told that he lacked any real creativity. With countless films, television networks, and theme parks, Walt Disney's work has become a childhood fixture across several generations. The Disney empire today is worth approximately $226 Billion.

Sergey Brin & Larry Page: When Larry Page and Sergey Brin created Google, they tried to sell it to a competitor for only $1 Million so they could return to graduate school. The competitor rejected the offer. Today, with over 70% of the market, Google is the world's #1 search engine. The Google brand is valued at $420 Billion.

Tom Brady: Tom Brady started his professional career as a 6th-round draft pick. Nonetheless, through consistent hard work, Brady has arguably become the greatest NFL quarterback of all time, with seven Super Bowl rings and five Super Bowl MVP awards. Tom Brady's net worth is an estimated $250 Million.

Jeff Bezos: Jeff Bezos often says it took billions of dollars in missteps to achieve great success. Despite setbacks like his company, Amazon nearly going bankrupt during the dot-com crash of 2000, Bezos is one of the richest people in the world. Amazon generates $1.29 Billion in sales every day and Jeff Bezos' net worth is $167.6 Billion.

Ferruccio Lamborghini: Ferruccio Lamborghini tried to advise Ferrari about the clutch on their cars, but was laughed out of the factory. He decided to create his own model, and today Lamborghini is one of the top luxury car brands. The Lamborghini brand's net worth is estimated at $12 Billion.

Dwayne 'The Rock' Johnson: The Rock made a failed attempt at professional football. He is now a professional wrestling icon (with over 10 championship titles) and the highest-paid actor in Hollywood with his films netting $10.5 Billion in sales globally. Dwayne Johnson's net worth is $800 Million.

Steve Harvey: After getting fired from several jobs, Steve Harvey started his comic career virtually homeless. Today, Harvey is considered one of the greatest comedians of all time and a prolific television host, having hosted *Family Feud* for 12 years. Steve Harvey's net worth is an estimated $200 Million.

Mark Cuban: Mark Cuban is quoted as saying that he failed at almost every job he's ever held. Nonetheless, Cuban went on to become a media tycoon, owning the Dallas Mavericks and powerhouse, 2929 Entertainment, as well as regularly appearing on ABC's *Shark Tank*. Mark Cuban's net worth is $4.7 Billion.

Serena Williams: Unlike a lot of child tennis prodigies, Serena Williams grew up with a working-class background, and many doubted her talent early on. With 23 Grand Slam titles and four Olympic gold medals, Williams is one of the greatest athletes of all time. Serena Williams' net worth is $260 Million.

Jay-Z: Jay-Z made it out of the Brooklyn projects by selling drugs only to become one of the most critically acclaimed rappers. With over 140 million records sold, 24 Grammys, and the most #1 albums on the Billboard 200, Jay-Z is one of the bestselling musicians of all time. His net worth is $1.3 Billion.

Kevin Hart: Kevin Hart failed at standup comedy for years. Through all the failure, he kept going, and is now one of the most prolific, commercially successful comedians, having released 5 comedy albums and starred in 58 films (and counting). Kevin Hart's net worth is $450 Million.

Ruth Fertel: As a single mom, Ruth Fertel set up her own successful restaurant that was tragically destroyed by a kitchen fire. Fertel later re-opened and re-named it, Ruth's Chris Steakhouse. Today there are Ruth's Chris Steakhouses in 21 countries, and the estimated net worth of the franchise is $42.28 Million.

Sara Blakely: Sara Blakely initially had dreams of becoming a lawyer. But after failing the LSATs, she changed career trajectories and eventually invented Spanx, a leading intimate wear brand. Sara Blakely's net worth is $1.1 Billion.

Samuel L. Jackson: Despite beginning his acting career at 24 years old, Samuel L. Jackson did not receive any notable roles until his 40's. Jackson has gone on to star in over 150 films. Netting $27 Billion at the box office, he is the highest-grossing lead actor of all time. Samuel L. Jackson's net worth is $250 Million.

Elvis Presley: As a child, Elvis Presley failed all his music classes. He went on to help radically transform the music industry as the "King of Rock 'n Roll," selling 400 million records across the world, and winning 3 Grammys. Presley's net worth at the time of his death was $5 Million (equates to $20 Million today).

Steve Jobs: After building Apple from the ground up, Steve Jobs was kicked out of his own company at the age of 30. He would return twelve years later and save Apple from bankruptcy with groundbreaking product launches like the iPod and the iPhone. The net worth of the Apple brand today is an estimated $65 Billion.

Benjamin Franklin: Ben Franklin came up with several failed political proposals and inventions. Nonetheless, he became one of the Founding Fathers of the United States of America, he is one of the authors of the Declaration of Independence, and his face is on the $100 bill.

Jerry Seinfeld: Jerry Seinfeld was booed off stage at his first standup gig. Despite this failure, he is not only one of the greatest standup comics of all time, but for nine years he starred in and co-wrote the hit comedy show, *Seinfeld,* which won 10 Primetime Emmys. Jerry Seinfeld's net worth is $950 Million.

Abraham Lincoln: Abraham Lincoln's political career was riddled with losses. Despite these failures, he eventually was elected to the presidency in 1860. With the leadership skills to keep a nation together amidst civil war, Lincoln is considered by a majority of historians to be the greatest U.S. president of all time.

Eminem: Eminem failed the 9th grade three times before dropping out. He went on to become one of the greatest rappers of all time with 10 #1 albums, 15 Grammys, an Academy Award, and over 220 million records sold worldwide. Eminem is worth $230 Million.

Soichiro Honda: Soichiro Honda's factory was bombed twice during WWII. Honda rebuilt the company from the ground up and turned it into one of the biggest car brands in the world, selling over a million cars in the U.S. in 2021 alone. The net worth of the Honda brand is an estimated $46.58 Billion.

George Lucas: George Lucas' idea for *Star Wars* was rejected by 3 different film studios. He used that rejection as motivation to turn his script into the iconic movie franchise it is today, grossing $70 Billion. George Lucas' net worth is $5.8 Billion.

Denzel Washington: Denzel Washington coined the phrase, "Fail forward" as a result of missteps he took in his childhood. Because of his perseverance, he is one of the greatest actors in the world with two Academy Awards, a Tony Award, and three Golden Globe Awards. Denzel Washington's net worth is $280 Million.

Lady Gaga: Lady Gaga was cut from her first record label. She didn't let this stop her from her dreams of becoming a pop star. Gaga has since sold 170 million records worldwide, won 13 Grammys, an Academy Award, and was recently inducted into the Songwriters Hall of Fame. Lady Gaga's net worth is $150 Million.

Ed Mylett: Ed Mylett went through several personal trials as a youth. Nonetheless, Mylett went on to lead various successful ventures from tech to real estate. He is the author of the bestseller, *#MaxOut Your Life* and he hosts the podcast, *The Ed Mylett Show.*

Arianna Huffington: Arianna Huffington was a failed author (with 36 publisher rejections) and failed politician (getting less than a percent of the vote in a bid for California Governor). Huffington went on to co-found well-respected news outlet, *The Huffington Post.* Arianna Huffington's net worth is $100 Million.

David Goggins: David Goggins grew up in an abusive household. Today he is a world-renowned public speaker and bestselling author.

Orville Wright & Wilbur Wright: It took the Wright Brothers years of failed plane prototypes before they revolutionized the travel industry by inventing and successfully flying the first motor-operated airplane.

Sir Isaac Newton: Sir Isaac Newton tried to run his family farm, and failed miserably. Today he is known as one of the key thinkers of the Enlightenment and the scientist behind the laws of motion and gravity.

Henry Ford: Investors backed out of Henry Ford's first vehicle. Despite the doubters, Ford would go on to introduce the Ford Model T to the world and change transportation forever. Henry Ford's net worth by today's standards would be an estimated $35.2 Billion.

Robert Downey Jr: Robert Downey Jr. struggled with alcohol and drug abuse for decades. Downey has now been sober for 19 years and has maintained an iconic acting career, starring in several box office smash hits like *Avengers: End Game* (2019). Robert Downey Jr.'s net worth is $300 Million.

Brian Chesky: When Brian Chesky shopped his idea for Airbnb around, he was turned down by seven investors. Chesky went on to completely shake up the hospitality industry with Airbnb. There are now 4 million Airbnb hosts all over the world. Brian Chesky's net worth is $9.7 Billion.

Colonel Harland Sanders: Colonel Sanders worked many odd jobs, including running a ferryboat company. He didn't discover his passion and his secret fried chicken recipe until his 60s. With the launch of Kentucky Fried Chicken (KFC), Colonel Sanders revolutionized the fast food industry. Today, the KFC brand's net worth is an estimated $10 Billion.

Vera Wang: In her adolescence, Vera Wang was a figure skater with aspirations for the Olympics. When she failed to qualify, she decided to work her way up in the fashion industry. Today, Wang is one of the top luxury fashion designers. Vera Wang's net worth is $650 Million.

Stephen Curry: Early in his career, critics doubted Stephen Curry's potential because of his height and size. As an eight-time NBA All-Star with four NBA championships and two MVP awards, Curry is already one of the greatest basketball players of all time. Stephen Curry's net worth is $160 Million.

Ed Sheeran: Ed Sheeran grew up with a stutter that he eventually learned to get rid of. Today, Sheeran is a prolific musician, writing hits for artists like Taylor Swift. He's sold 150 million records worldwide, and he was the second most streamed artist of the 2010s. Ed Sheeran's net worth is $200 Million.

The Beatles: The Beatles bombed their audition with their first prospective record label. They would eventually sign with Polydor Records and go on to become the greatest rock band of all time selling 600 million albums worldwide, making 20 #1 hits, and earning seven Grammys.

James Dyson: It took over 5,000 failed prototypes for James Dyson to eventually come up with the famed Dyson vacuum, the world's first bagless vacuum. Today, Dyson vacuums are used all over the world. James Dyson's net worth is $7.7 Billion.

Joe Rogan: Joe Rogan started as a struggling stand-up comedian. Nonetheless, he's done countless standup specials and television host spots. His podcast show, *The Joe Rogan Experience*, was recently bought by Spotify for $100 Million. Joe Rogan's net worth is $120 Million.

Richard Branson: Richard Branson has had many business failures in several industries, from fashion to cars. Regardless of these missteps, he's created eight different billion-dollar companies in eight different countries, most notably one of the top record labels in the world, Virgin Records. Richard Branson's net worth is $4.2 Billion.

Sheryl Sandberg: Sheryl Sandberg helped popularize the phrase, "Fail fast," as she's taken some well publicized missteps in her career. Nonetheless Sandberg played a pivotal role in expanding Meta (formally Facebook) from 500 employees and 100 million users in 2008 to well over 70,000 employees and 3 billion users. Sandberg's net worth is $1.5 Billion.

Chris Gardner: Chris Gardner was forced to live on the streets with his son for a year. Gardner is now the CEO and founder of Christopher Gardner International Holdings, a public speaker, and the inspiration for the Oscar-nominated film, *The Pursuit of Happyness* (2006). Chris Gardner is worth $70 Million.

Howard Schultz: When Howard Schultz shopped his idea for Starbucks around, he was rejected by 24 different firms for funding. Schultz still persevered and built one of the biggest coffee empires in the world. There are over 33,000 Starbucks all over the world. And the net worth of the Starbucks brand is an estimated $52.83 Billion.

Stan Lee: Stan Lee wouldn't make his first breakthrough comic, 1962's *Amazing Fantasy Fifteen* (the first feature of Spiderman) until he was 40. He would go on to create an entire comic universe that is still being turned into box office hits today. Stan Lee's net worth at his death was $50 Million.

I hope these stories inspire you to never give up no matter what failures or obstacles you face. Embrace rejection and failure as a necessary part of your journey to success in tech sales.

Just as these iconic people have done, use your *setbacks* as *setups* for unstoppable success.

PART 3

THE MATH

The next thing you need to learn to get a job in tech sales is what I like to call:

THE SIX-FIGURE SALES MATH

This is the math and activity required to land your dream job in tech sales.

The sales math is critical for your success because you need to understand all the leads, appointments, and job offers that are required for success!

To do the six-figure sales math, you first need to learn the elements of a sales funnel.

A sales funnel is a visual representation of the buyer's journey.

When we break down your sales funnel for your job search, there are 3 core elements:

#1) Leads

#2) Interviews

#3) Job Offers

- **Leads** are the amount of contacts and companies you put in a list and prospect for a tech sales job.

- **Interviews** are the amount of interviews you have for different jobs.

- **Job offers** are the amount of job offers you receive from different companies to get hired.

On average, leads convert to interviews at 2.5% - 10%. The term for this in the tech industry is called "conversion rate."

This means if you are prospecting 100 leads for a tech sales job, you can expect to book 3 - 10 interviews out of 100 (2.5% - 10% x 100 = 3 - 10 interviews).

I always like to be as conservative as possible and assume the worst-case scenario, so feel free to use the lower end of the scale and expect to book around two interviews for every 100 leads you prospect for a job.

Next, you need to understand the conversion rate from interviews to job offers.

The conversion rate from interviews to job offers (in other words, the number of interviews you have that turn into job offers) typically ranges from 20% - 40%. This all depends on how well you do with prospecting, pitching, and closing in the sales process to get your tech sales job.

Let's say for this scenario, you prospected 100 leads and booked 10 interviews.

If you had 10 interviews on the calendar, you can expect to convert at 20% - 40% conversion rate which would result in 2 - 4 job offers.

LEADS	100 LEADS
CONVERSION RATE	10%
INTERVIEWS	10 INTERVIEWS
CONVERSION RATE	20%
JOB OFFERS	2

If you study the secrets in this book for your job search, you will be able to increase your conversion rates at every stage of the sales funnel from leads to interviews, and interviews to job offers.

Now that you understand your six-figure sales math, you can manage your sales funnel for landing your dream tech sales job!

Your goal every day when prospecting for a tech sales job should be to prospect more leads at the top of the funnel, book more interviews at the middle of the funnel, and get more job offers at the bottom of the funnel.

Every day wake up and try to beat the amount of leads you prospected and interviews you had from the day before.

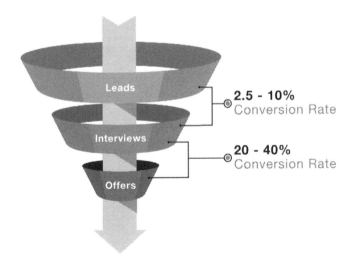

The more leads you prospect at the top of the funnel, the more interviews and job offers you will get at the bottom of the funnel.

Using the funnel and conversion rate examples previously mentioned, if you went from prospecting 100 leads a day to prospecting 200 leads a day, you can estimate that you would book 20 interviews (10% x 200 leads = 20 interviews) and you would get 4 job offers (20% x 10 interviews = 4 offers).

Every day you will want to track your six-figure sales math data and work to improve your activity and conversion rates of your sales funnel.

The more activity and hard work you put into getting a job in tech sales, the more leads, interviews, and job offers you will get!

Claim your FREE Bonus Bundle

GIVE BACK

If the secrets in this book have helped you out in any way, take 60 seconds out to write a review: **www.amzn.to/3Yki4qT**

Your review makes it easier for all the aspiring sales reps out there to see this book and get the secrets they need to jumpstart their career.

Write a review, screenshot it, and upload it at:

www.BrandonBornancin.com/techsalesbonus

And we will grant you access to our bonus bundle.

These bonuses will help you crush every stage of the job application process, from sending a resume to signing an offer.

If you please take just a minute out of your day to leave a review (that's less than the time you spend scrolling through social media, admit it!), you'll get access to everything you need to land your dream job faster than ever.

Thank you so much for doing your part to pay it forward and help spread the word about *The Ultimate Guide To Breaking Into Tech Sales.*

Scan to Write a Review & Claim Bonuses!

Total Value: $1,935

www.BrandonBornancin.com/techsalesbonus

Now let's get back to your job hunt journey.

PART 4

THE MARKETING

DOCUMENT ALL YOUR ACCOMPLISHMENTS & SKILLS

When people think of marketing, what comes to mind are billboards, glossy magazine ads, and witty commercials.

But when you apply for a job, you're marketing yourself to the employers. And how good or bad you can market yourself (your skills, your abilities, the results you drive) will determine the odds of you getting hired.

If you want to get a dream tech sales job, you're going to have to learn how to market yourself well.

You want to have a strong LinkedIn profile, a solid resume, and a great cover letter (that cuts through the noise). And you always want to dress your best.

Before you get started with the marketing and branding tasks I will have you complete, I need you to take an inventory of the following in a Google doc. You're going to take the information that you provide for each of these categories and repurpose it for all the marketing you will do for yourself. This way, if you are looking to update your social media page or preparing for a meet-up with a sales department leader, you don't have to scramble to think of what to write or say. You will have everything you need in this single Google doc.

ACCOMPLISHMENTS

What have you achieved so far in your professional life that you are the proudest of?

What big accomplishments have you achieved at every single job you've had?

Don't be shy here. This is the space to brag about yourself and how much more amazing you are than every other job candidate out there. Sell yourself to the recruiter.

SKILLS

What soft skills and hard skills do you have that would be an asset at a sales job?

Hard skills are usually job-specific abilities that can be measured and quantified.

Whereas soft skills are typically interpersonal abilities that can't necessarily be measured.

Examples of soft skills include:

- Excellent communication skills

- A good work ethic

- Being a lifelong learner

- Thriving under pressure

- Tenacity

- Coachability

- Being a team player

Examples of hard skills for sales include:

- Research

- Product knowledge

- Objection handling

- Prospecting

- Pitching

- Closing

- Qualifying leads

AWARDS & ACCOLADES

What awards at school or previous jobs have you won?

Have you won "Employee of the Month" or any department-specific awards?

If you've worked a sales job before, have you received accolades for being a top earner of the month or the quarter?

Back in school, were you ever on the Dean's List? Did you receive any scholarships (academic, athletic, etc.)?

Awards will give a recruiter a sense of how exceptional you are, as well as the quality and excellence you can bring to an organization.

PROJECTS

What big projects have you completed at past jobs?

What were the goals and objectives?

What was the outcome?

What impact did the project have on the organization's bottom line?

Projects can give a recruiter a glimpse into the results you can drive.

This is a great opportunity to illustrate your project management skills, organizational skills, and time management. Plus projects illustrate to a recruiter that you have the dedication to see long-term goals through to the end without quitting.

FAILURES

While you don't want to frontload failures in your resume or any other application materials, during the interview process you may be prompted to discuss a time that you failed at something.

All of us have lots of mistakes and failures we could mention in an interview, but you want to be strategic with the failure story you choose. In other words, choose a story that allows you to highlight a valuable lesson you learned and can therefore bring with you to this new company.

For instance, maybe you had a group project that didn't yield the outcomes that you expected, but this failure and experience gave you insights into the market or it taught you how to work with and manage different personalities.

Be strategic about the failure you share, and highlight the lesson you learned.

In addition to these categories and questions, I would also list out the professional and personal challenges you had to overcome. Maybe your first year of college was particularly rough because of a personal challenge, but you persevered. Or perhaps you faced L after L at work, but you still had to muster up the drive to hit a goal or a project hard and crush it.

These types of stories are great to have on hand because they illustrate the grit that you have to make it through tough times. And this is a quality that you can't train anyone on. Top employers love to find and hire people who exude tenacity and passion to persevere through anything.

Once you document all of your skills and accomplishments, you're ready to move on to building your LinkedIn page and your social media presence.

HIRE A PHOTOGRAPHER

A good amount of sourcing for jobs happens on social media platforms like LinkedIn. Hiring managers look through hundreds of profiles a day of candidates in their area. On top of that, if your application gets selected, and you become a job candidate, employers will visit your LinkedIn profile and social media profiles to research you before they hire you.

Because your profile picture is one of the first things people see, I would advise you to hire a photographer and get professional headshots done.

Hiring a photographer can be a bit pricey, I get it. It sounds like a luxury and something completely unnecessary, but this is the best way to guarantee that you're making a positive first impression.

You may not be in tech sales yet, but you want to look the part and play the part. You have to fake it till you make it. And if you don't have a professional headshot for your LinkedIn profile, you won't look the part of a tech sales genius.

Additionally, since you'll be doing a lot of job prospecting and setting up meetings through LinkedIn, a nice headshot can make the difference between someone ignoring your message and scrolling past you, or deciding to learn more about you because they were influenced by your professional photo.

There are countless places you can go to book a photographer. You can hire someone off Craigslist. You can just drop an ad for a photographer who does headshots. You can also look through LinkedIn.

And if the price is a concern and you don't want to fork over several hundred dollars (I totally understand) you can try Upwork. Upwork is a great resource where you can find a photographer for whatever price range you have. There are also virtual headshot services (i.e. Snapbar Studio), where you dress up, take a photo of yourself, send it in, and a designer will edit your photo (change the background, adjust the lighting, etc.) and make it look like a professional headshot for less than $100.

With these different resources, there's no reason why you can't get a headshot done. So whatever you do, don't try to take a selfie in your apartment or have your mom take a picture of you, and use that as your profile. Making the extra effort here goes a long way.

In addition to headshots, you may want to consider having some professional photos taken of you "on the job" working so you can post these on your social media feeds. These live-action shots aren't necessary, but the headshot is a must.

HIRE A DESIGNER FOR YOUR COVER PHOTO

In addition to a profile picture, on LinkedIn, you will also have a cover photo. The cover photo is essentially a banner that sits right behind your profile picture.

A cover photo doesn't grab as much attention and make as big of an impression as a profile picture, but it does contribute to the overall vibe of your page.

With a cover photo, you have the freedom to showcase more of your personality with a live-action photo of yourself. It can be a staged action shot that you take with your photographer. Or you can use a picture of yourself on the job, at a networking event, giving a presentation, shaking hands with an influencer in tech sales, etc.

In addition to action photos, you can also use your cover photo to highlight your professional and personal goals (i.e. "To start a career in tech sales," "To help the company that hires me make millions in software sales," etc.), your core values, your mission, your vision, or your belief statements. This way anyone who views your cover photo on LinkedIn will be super impressed with your professionalism and your intentions. A cover photo that shows this value will let a hiring manager know that if they take the risk and invest in your success (yes, hiring managers always see it as a risk to hire an entry-level salesperson because there's a chance the new rep won't want to be in sales), you will provide them with outstanding returns.

Lastly, make it easy for people who contact you to schedule an interview by including your phone number and email on your cover photo. You can even create a QR code business card using free apps like Blinq.me for when you're out and about networking in person.

If you use your cover photo to showcase that you are all in on tech sales, and you will do whatever it takes to work hard and exceed job expectations…

I guarantee you will get the job offer over someone randomly applying with an amateur-looking LinkedIn page.

HIRE A DESIGNER FOR ALL YOUR MARKETING NEEDS

I mentioned in previous sections to hire a photographer to take headshots. To make your marketing and self-promotion more competitive, I would advise you to hire a designer.

Depending on how intricate you want to make your cover photo (whether you want to do a combination of imagery and text), a designer can easily bring whatever vision you have to life and make your cover photo as attention-grabbing as possible.

While you are at it, I recommend having the designer create professional cover photos for other social media sites that may be reviewed by potential employers.

Even though you're going to do a majority of your networking online, you still may run into important people at networking events, and therefore you'll need a good business card to pass out. While everyone else is using generic templates like Vistaprint, a designer can come up with a design that reflects your unique personality.

Another way you can stand out from the crowd is with a personal website. A personal website is one of the easiest ways to make a great impression with a recruiter because it's an extra step that most people don't take.

In addition to the content you provide (resume, bio, results you've delivered, etc.) a designer can put together a polished website that balances professionalism and your personality so that when hiring managers look you up, you have total control over what comes up.

Just like the photographer, a designer may sound like an unnecessary expense, but all these efforts add up and let the hiring manager know how serious you are about getting the job and becoming a top earner in tech sales.

The more you invest in your success, the more success you will get.

The more you pay, the more people will pay you.

LINKEDIN PROFILE REDESIGN

To get a job in tech sales and make over $100,000 a year, you need to have a top 1% LinkedIn profile.

To have the best LinkedIn profile that stands out from the crowd, separates you from the sheep, and helps you land your dream tech sales job as fast as possible...

Hire an expert LinkedIn profile writer to update your profile.

You can find a freelance writer on LinkedIn or you can do a simple Google search (i.e. "LinkedIn profile writer"). Additionally, you can look for talent on sites like TopResume, LinkedIn ProFinder, and Find My Profession.

Typically, the cost for a LinkedIn profile writer can range from $100 to $500, depending on what you have them do. Often, if you have them write additional documents like your resume, these extra projects will drive up the cost.

But honestly, if you're having a professional writer put together your profile, and other application documents that you'll end up re-using several times, saving yourself the time and the headache of putting these materials together yourself is well worth the extra cost.

On top of that, a seasoned professional writer who's put together several profiles is going to know what works and what doesn't work. They will have a deep understanding of the content, the layout, the design, etc. that's going to best illustrate your talents, help you stand out, and command the attention of recruiters and hiring managers.

There are countless benefits to hiring a profile writer, but if you can't come up with the cash to invest in your success, then you can always do it on your own.

Your LinkedIn profile should have a professional profile picture and a cover photo (which were both covered in the previous sections). In addition to this, your profile should also include:

LINKEDIN HEADLINE

Right underneath your name is your headline, one of the most visible sections of your profile.

The headline is prime real estate on your profile page. Yet I see so many people waste this space on generic information like their job title, where they work, or their educational background.

You want to make the most out of this space, which means instead of regurgitating generic info, you want to frontload the value you bring to the table and the potential you have to become a key player in the sales industry.

In addition to presenting value, you also want to be strategic about the words you choose in your headline and keep LinkedIn's search algorithm in mind. In other words, select keywords that a hiring manager looking for a tech sales rep would use.

Examples:

- Sales and Sales Management Major graduating in May 2023 and looking for a full-time sales position.

- {{Your current position}} at {{company}} focused on carving out a long-term career in tech sales.

LINKEDIN SUMMARY

Think of the summary or "About" section as the long form of your LinkedIn headline. This is where you add strength and personality to your profile by telling your career story.

What have you accomplished professionally up to this point? What training and education have you completed?

Paint a picture for the profile viewers and describe to them the trajectory that your career has taken. Where do you want to go from here? Most importantly, how can you help potential employers (because the job hunt is all about what you can do for others)?

The "About" section is the easiest way to set yourself apart from the millions of other job applicants out there, so take your time here, and inject your personality into this section.

Just like with your headline, keywords from your summary are picked up by LinkedIn's algorithm and will strengthen your searchability. So be mindful of what recruiters are searching for and be sure to include those key terms in your "About" section in a way that is natural (of course) and not forced or obvious. One of the easiest ways to figure out the keywords hiring managers are searching for is to pull up a job advertisement for a tech sales rep. Then integrate any applicable key terms into your "About" section.

Lastly, leave a call to action towards the end asking people to connect and reach out to you.

LINKEDIN EXPERIENCE

Showcasing your professional journey on LinkedIn is how you can stand out to recruiters, potential connections, and customers.

In this section, it's important to not just include the last five jobs you've had. You want to also include any freelance work you've done, side hustles, volunteer time, projects – really anything beyond day-to-day work so that hiring managers can get a better picture of who you are as a working professional and as a well-rounded, developed person.

Here are a few ways you can strengthen your LinkedIn "Experience" section:

- Link your job to the company you work for. This helps give context and builds credibility.

- Instead of using passive language like, "I was a salesperson at Company X," use action words that describe the work you did like "managed," "led," "grew," "reduced," "saved," and "sold."

- Paint a picture of what you did at each position (daily tasks, challenges, wins). Don't just list job titles.

- Use keywords. Similar to the headline and summary sections keywords still apply and boost your searchability. Research the keywords that you should include for each job or position by reviewing the job ads you're going after.

- Be clear and concise. If you can say something in fewer words, choose the less wordy option.

- Spotlight your achievements effectively. Instead of saying "Promoted to {{current position}} where I increased company revenue by 14% in my first year." Instead try, "Increased sales revenue by 14% in the first year following my promotion to {{current position}}." Spotlight the achievement and follow up with the title or position.

- With everything you write, but especially with your profile, always check your spelling and grammar. Typos are unprofessional and make a bad impression.

- Add supplemental materials (PDFs, PowerPoint presentations, etc.) to vet what you say in the "Experience" section.

LINKEDIN SKILLS

The "Skills & Endorsements" section showcases what you are qualified to do at a glance.

The featured "Skills & Endorsements" section is a great way to demonstrate the unique skill set you provide. Anytime someone on LinkedIn "endorses" one of your listed skills, it adds credibility to your profile.

Keep in mind that this section is not about listing as many skills as you can. It's about being strategic and listing skills that are relevant to a tech sales career.

Below are a few of the most desired skills to have on your LinkedIn profile if you're looking to get into tech sales:

- Cold Calling

- Sales Emailing

- Social Selling

- Prospecting

- Appointment Setting

- Pipeline Management

- CRM

- Persuasion

- Critical Thinking

- Problem Solving

- Adaptability

- Time Management

- Tenacity

- Emotional Acumen

- People Management

- Analytical Reasoning

- Creativity

- Data-Driven Decision Making

HIRE A RESUME WRITER

When I was in college at Ohio University, before my startup took off, I hired an expert resume writer.

I believe the service cost me $125 total for two resume versions and a professional cover letter.

Once I paid for the service, she interviewed me and asked me questions about my background and experience. She looked over my list of past jobs and accomplishments that I provided, and then put together one of the most professional resumes that I could have ever imagined.

This resume perfectly encapsulated what I'd been able to accomplish up until that point, my relevant skills, and talents, as well as my potential – which can all be challenging with resume writing.

There was no way in hell I would have been able to do what she did. On top of that, it only took her a few days to write this resume, so the turnaround time was incredibly fast.

So when it comes to putting together a resume, my first advice to you is to hire a resume writer.

One of the keys to success in sales and life is to not only find out what you need to do to achieve your goals but when you come across tasks that require skill sets you don't have, hire the people who have those strengths to help you get the job done.

This is why I hired a resume writer and you need to as well.

Hiring a resume writer will give you the best chance of success in the job market. A professional writer will help you stand out from the crowd, showcase you as the best talent investment any employer can make for their tech sales position, and they will help you get more interviews faster than ever before.

For resources on how to hire a resume writer, try freelancing platforms like Upwork or resume writing companies like TopResume. You can also search on LinkedIn for resume writers, ask around, or look at hiring contractors.

And when you get ready to choose a writer, only hire a resume writer who has written at least 25 resumes and has at least five years of experience.

Ask to see their resume because you'll want to verify that they have the education and the credentials to do the job.

Most importantly, ask for samples of their work and make sure that they are well-versed in tech sales. You want to make sure you are hiring someone who has written tech sales resumes before, knows the ins and outs of the industry, as well as what an employer is looking for in an entry or mid-level tech sales rep.

The writer I hired had hundreds of resumes and was a guru at her craft.

You want to look for the same.

And if you just don't have the money to hire a resume writer, that's ok.

Your next best bet is to write your resume yourself.

Your resume should include the following:

OBJECTIVE STATEMENT

At the top of your resume, you should have a FIRE objective statement. Think of your objective statement as a two to three-sentence pitch, where you are selling the hiring manager on you, and why they should choose you for the job.

A great objective statement encapsulates who you are as a professional, the results you've delivered at past jobs, the impact you can drive at the job you're applying for, the "secret sauce" that separates you from the pack, and what you're looking for in a job.

Here's an example of an objective statement for an entry-level tech sales job:

Highly driven college graduate with 4+ years of retail sales experience, a track record of crushing quota month after month, and turning passive "window shoppers" into top 1% clients. With my educational background, I thrive in high-pressure environments, and I have an innate ability to act as both a team player and a self-starter who can problem-solve independently. Currently seeking an entry-level tech sales position with opportunities for advancement in a lifelong sales career.

PROFESSIONAL EXPERIENCE

List out any relevant work experience you have (over the last 10 years). And for each job, highlight the skills and daily tasks you completed that are relevant to a tech sales job.

Maybe you worked for a retail chain at your local mall, and you had a sales quota every month to meet – that's relevant experience.

Or maybe in high school, you were a manager at a restaurant – that's leadership experience that you can bring to a tech sales job!

Maybe you didn't work a job during school, but you picked up strong organizational skills that are crucial to a successful tech sales career.

My point here is that you have way more relevant professional experience than you think. Make sure you include any and everything.

SALES SKILLS

Depending on how much work experience you have, you want to list out 5 to 20 professional skills (hard and soft) you have that are relevant to a tech sales position.

Some sales skills that may apply to you include:

- Strong communication skills

- Expertise with Google Workspace, Microsoft Office Suite , etc.

- Tech proficiency

- Time management

- Team player

- Passion for excellence

- Detail-oriented

Whenever a hiring manager fills a position, there's always a risk that things won't work out for whatever reason, and they're back at square one with an empty seat.

In the "Achievements" section, kill that doubt by showcasing your track record of excellence.

Relevant achievements you could include are:

- # of times you've met or crushed quota

- # of sales you've closed

- The revenue you've generated for past employers

- Scholarships

- Awards

- Employee of the month wins

If you want to get paid, you have to pay the price!

So again, my advice for you is to hire the best resume writer, because they will articulate your talent and potential the most effectively.

However, if you can't hire a writer, then these are the essential sections you want to nail in your resume.

Unless you are applying for higher-level manager or executive roles later on in your career, as a general rule of thumb, your resume should be no longer than a page.

And if you want to reference additional books to make sure you produce the strongest resume possible, consider…

- **Richard N. Bolles' *What Color Is Your Parachute?***

In What Color Is Your Parachute? Bolles helps you identify your work-related strengths and weaknesses, so you know what to play up in your resume and what to work around. For instance, if you learn from this book that you're a big procrastinator, instead of mentioning that in a resume or an interview, discuss how well you work and thrive under pressure (see what we did there?). *What Color is Your Parachute?* is full of advice for embracing your greatest assets.

- **Dan Clay's** *How to Write the Perfect Resume: Stand Out, Land Interviews, and Get the Job You Want*

Clay breaks down how to play up your greatest achievements and shares his tested and proven system for writing an exceptional resume that cuts through the noise and helps you land an interview.

COVER LETTER

In addition to a resume, you will also need a cover letter.

A cover letter is a one-pager where you introduce yourself to the hiring manager and provide a summary of your professional experience that's going to entice the hiring manager to read your resume.

Within the seconds it takes to read a cover letter, a recruiter or hiring manager will decide if they want to keep reading or delete your application forever, so you want to really wow them with the value you bring to the table.

Even though a cover letter is a bit old school, many jobs will still ask you to attach one along with your resume. Even if a job doesn't explicitly ask you to include a cover letter, putting together a doc like this to attach shows how serious you are and your willingness to go the extra mile to impress the employer.

When it comes to writing a cover letter, just like with the resume, I would advise you to have a writer put together a cover letter. In fact, once you hire a resume writer to write and redesign your resume, ask them if they can also help you write a cover letter.

Since they will essentially become an expert on your background and your accomplishments, by the time they're done with your resume, they should be able to easily put together a strong cover letter.

And if you can't afford to hire a writer to draft a cover letter for you, then you can of course write your own.

Your cover letter should be formatted like a standard letter, with the date and the contact information (name, title, company, address) of the person you're writing to listed towards the top with some kind of greeting (i.e. "Dear Mrs. Jones," etc.).

In addition to these basics, make sure your cover letter also includes:

- **An introductory paragraph** that briefly explains how you heard about the job opportunity. Was it through a mutual contact? Did you read about it on LinkedIn? Or maybe you found the company on your own and pitched them for a sales rep job? Also explain why you want the job. Remember, even when you're talking about what you want, you should still make it about the manager and the company. How can you make a positive impact at this organization?

- **Second and third paragraphs** that summarize the experience you have and connect the dots for the hiring manager. In other words, explain how the hard and soft skills you have set you apart from other applicants and make you a perfect fit. Get creative with how you summarize your experience and describe a specific problem you solved at a past job. Whatever you decide, keep in mind that these paragraphs should be no more than 5 sentences each (you only have a page to work with altogether) so pick the strongest examples and stories you've got to showcase your abilities.

- **A closing** where you thank the reader for their time and consideration, provide a follow-up date (this communicates that you're serious), and your contact information.

Again, I would advise you to hire a professional writer to put together your resume and your cover letter. It may sound unnecessary, but it's an investment in landing your dream six-figure tech sales job.

If you want to get into tech sales, you can't make excuses to achieve success... you have to work for it and do whatever it takes.

But if you have no way of getting together the money to do this, then these are the points you want to make sure you hit in your cover letter.

SOCIAL PROOF & TESTIMONIALS

In addition to your LinkedIn profile and your resume, one of the best ways to sell yourself to potential employers is to let other people brag about how amazing you are and the impact you've made.

Think about it... If you were a prospect looking for a software product, what would sell you faster?

Would me telling you how much money you can make if you use my sales software Seamless.AI, sell you?

Or would thousands of people telling you how they used the Seamless. AI software to make millions in new sales sell you?

Which would be more convincing?

Of course testimonials are always going to win you over because when you hear people share their success with a product, that social proof sells you faster than a salesperson discussing how great their product is so they get their commission.

A testimonial is more persuasive than a sales pitch because the person giving a testimonial has nothing to gain or lose by sharing their story. They simply came across a product that changed their life, and they want you to know about it so you can see the same results.

The persuasive power of testimonials is one of the reasons why I collected videos and written testimonials from my top customers, and displayed them at:

www.PresidentsClubAwards.com/application

Testimonials sell, but they don't just apply to software or weight loss products.

That's right. You can leverage testimonials as you hunt for a tech sales job.

In fact, you should make it a habit to start collecting testimonials right now at every job you ever worked.

Any time you work for anyone or accomplish a big milestone at a job, keep an ongoing list in a Google doc of the results you achieved, as well as written testimonials or video testimonials from clients, leaders, and co-workers who can detail the value you delivered for them.

And if you can get these people to write a recommendation for you to post on your LinkedIn profile, that's even better!

Then, you can drop your social proof with anyone you interview with, and this will help give you a competitive edge.

If you already have people in mind who could testify to the wins you drive, but you're not sure how to ask them for a testimonial (this can be an awkward request to make. I don't blame you), try out these scripts.

SCRIPTS TO LEVERAGE TESTIMONIALS

Subject Line: {{Your Name}} Job Recommendation

Hi {{First_name}} – I learned so much working for you! It was truly a pleasure.

I'm reaching out because I'm applying for a job in tech sales to take my career to the next level, and I wanted to know if I could get a recommendation from you.

Could you share in a quick iPhone video or by replying here your experience working with me?

Feel free to share as much detail as you want. Or if you only have the time to send something on the shorter side that's completely fine too. Everything helps!

I want anyone who interviews me for a job to understand from others my work ethic and the investment I make in the people I work for.

Again, your help is truly appreciated.

Thank you!

{{your_name}}
{{your_email}}
{{your_cell number}}

Once you have some social proof of your excellence from past employers, here is how I would give a list of testimonials to a potential employer interviewing me for a job:

Subject Line: {{Your Name}} Testimonials

Hi {{first_name}} – I wanted to share some social proof from people I've worked with in the past.

One of my sales mentors taught me that I can try to do all the selling or I can let all of my customers do the selling for me with their testimonials…

With this in mind, I hope the list of recommendations below gives you a better picture of who I am and what I will bring to the table to help you and your team achieve all your goals.

Thank you and I look forward to working for you!

Name
Title
Company
Testimonial

Name
Title
Company
Testimonial

Name
Title
Company
Testimonial

{{your_name}}
{{your_email}}
{{your_cell number}}

MARKETING DRESS CODE

Whether you're going to an interview in person, doing a virtual interview, or meeting a sales leader or recruiter just to discuss a job opportunity, always follow this rule:

Dress for the $100K tech sales job you want, not the job you have.

Let's say you have Candidate A vs Candidate B interviewing.

Candidate A shows up looking neat, but they're casually dressed in sneakers, jeans, and a t-shirt.

Candidate B by contrast shows up dressed to the nines. They're wearing slacks, a blouse or dress shirt, a blazer, and dress shoes.

Both candidates have the same education, job history, and experience.

Which candidate do you think gets the job?

Of course, it's going to be Candidate B every time.

We're all raised to not "judge a book by its cover." But guess what? Everyone judges the damn book by the cover. The books with the best covers outsell 98% of the other books in their category because the damn book cover matters and it's the thing that draws people in.

The same goes for you and how you present yourself.

In an interview, they're judging and evaluating everything about you, from the time you drive into the parking garage (yes, sometimes this is the case with companies) to the time you leave.

What you wear matters and you want to know why? Because when you work for a company, you are a representation of that company. And most businesses don't want their brand to be represented to the world in jeans and a t-shirt.

Your appearance lets employers know how seriously you are taking the job opportunity, and how badly you want it.

If you aren't going to take the extra effort to dress sharply, then they aren't going to take the effort to consider you for a job.

It's harsh to say, but if you look like shit, you will end up with a shitty job.

There are plenty of articles out there about the specific colors you should wear to an interview, whether you should wear heels or flats, whether or not you should blow your budget on an expensive suit or not, etc. None of that matters and you don't have to overthink what you wear.

As long as you dress professionally, wear neat clothes, clean shoes, and practice good hygiene, all of this will increase your chances of getting hired for a job in tech sales.

I have a motto for anyone that works with us and that is:

Dress for success!

Never forget that it's always better to show up to an interview overdressed than underdressed because that only lets the employer know that you care about getting the job.

And here's one bonus tip for this section: Don't wait for an interview, to dress nicely. Dress for success every time you go out because you never know who you will run into.

I've hired people I've met at parties, networking events, country clubs, you name it because they presented themselves professionally.

So always dress for success.

SOCIAL MEDIA CLEAN-UP

Before any employer hires you, I can guarantee you they will do a lot of research on you.

They're going to check out your LinkedIn and all your social media pages. They're going to google you and they will likely run a background check on you to search for any criminal history.

With this in mind, you will want to make sure that your social media presence is cleaned up and set up for success.

Do you have a lot of party pics? Get rid of them.

Do you have old accounts from high school that you wouldn't want popping up on a Google search? Deactivate them.

Do you talk a lot about politics, religion, or any other topics that most would deem controversial? Get rid of this, and make it a point from here on out to save those topics for in-person conversations instead of blasting your opinions all over your newsfeed or worse, getting into fights online with people. Your dream tech sales job just isn't worth engaging in a nasty back-and-forth with someone you will never meet in real life, so don't do it.

Many employers judge a book by its cover, and part of how they evaluate a job candidate is by looking at their social media presence.

If they hire you, you are going to become an extension of the company and the brand. Rather than risk tainting their brand by hiring someone with drunk college party pics or someone who's a cyberbully they are going to go with the candidate who has a track record for presenting dignity, class, and professionalism at all times.

If I had to choose between someone who looks like a party animal on Facebook with a few years of relevant work experience vs. someone whose social media is professional, but they lack work experience, I'm going to pick the more polished candidate. This is because the polished candidate is going to represent our brand in a positive light. More importantly, their professionalism shows all the potential they have.

You never want your social media presence to give off the vibe that you are "too risky" to hire. So clean it up and get rid of any pictures, videos, or posts that are inappropriate or controversial.

More importantly, get into the mindset of elevating and using your social media pages as outlets for professionalism, networking, and sales community building.

If you want to get a job in tech sales making $100,000 a year you have to act the job, look the job, and be the job. Doing a social media clean-up is a crucial part of this effort.

PART 5

THE TOOLS

T o get a job in tech sales and make $100,000 a year… you need to get all the best tools that the best salespeople use to generate millions in sales.

Not only will these powerful platforms make job hunting and prospecting easier, but once you start your tech sales job, these technologies will make your day-to-day tasks much easier.

In this section of *The Ultimate Guide To Breaking Into Tech Sales,* I will show you all the tools you need to succeed in tech sales, as well as a brief description of each tool.

If you need more training on how to master using these platforms, please search for tutorials on YouTube or Google. I want to keep this book as concise as possible to give you everything you need, without going down a rabbit hole on any individual topic.

The sales tools that you need to succeed are the following:

SEAMLESS.AI – THE WORLD'S BEST SALES LEADS

Seamless is the #1 sales software in the world that uses artificial intelligence to find accurate emails and cell phones for any professional in seconds.

Seamless won't just be vital for all your prospecting and list-building efforts when you start your sales job, but it will also help you score the perfect job.

With over 1.9 billion verified contact and company records, Seamless will give you access to a seemingly endless number of professional contacts.

So if you're interested in reaching the head of the sales team at a small to midsize business or Fortune 500 company, Seamless will have their cell phone and email address.

If you're trying to get a hold of the hiring manager at a local tech startup in your neighborhood, you'll be able to contact them through Seamless.

And if you want to get in front of more tech sales recruiters, Seamless will help you do just that.

To start using Seamless today, all you have to do is visit **www.seamless.ai**, click "Get Started Free," and start searching for contacts.

To find HR people and sales leaders, type in the search criteria for the target you're looking for (target company, target persona, geographic location, etc.). Then it will show you all the contacts and accounts that match your search.

When you join Seamless for free you will get $100 in credits (a credit essentially equals a lead or a person/business you can connect with).

And as a special bonus, if you write a review on Amazon for this book and upload a screenshot at:

www.BrandonBornancin.com/techsalesbonus

We'll add $250 in credits to your account to give you more "at bats" with finding the contact information of key sales leaders and hiring managers at any company.

CRM

A CRM is so crucial to staying organized with your job prospecting and sales efforts, but if you're new to tech sales, you're probably wondering… What exactly is a CRM?

CRM stands for "Customer Relationship Management" software.

There are a ton of different YouTube videos out there that can break down what a CRM is, but for the sake of being brief, I'm going to give you a cut-and-dry definition here…

A CRM helps you keep track of your leads, contacts, accounts, and opportunities, as well as the tasks you need to complete with each contact.

For example, let's say you meet someone about a job opportunity at a job fair. Instead of trying to remember their name, their contact information, and the next steps you should take with them on your own (let's face it, that's a lot to remember and you're going to end up forgetting something), a CRM will keep track of all this.

You just add that contact into the CRM, like this:

- First Name

- Last Name

- Title

- Company

- Email

- Cellphone

- Notes

- Task

- Task Due Date

As far as tasks go, the first task you would want to complete with the job fair contact is to send a "Thank you" email. Once that's done, you would check off that task in your CRM, and move on to the next step, which is scheduling an interview. And eventually, check that off and move on to the step after that.

A CRM will help you stay organized so that every day when you wake up, you will log into your CRM and complete all your open tasks associated with your leads and contacts.

And when you start your tech sales job, you will go from using a CRM every day of the week to keep up with job application processes to using it for list-building, prospecting, appointment setting, and closing sales.

As far as which CRM you end up choosing, I highly recommend signing up for the CRM that will most likely be used at your tech sales job, so this way you're killing two birds with one stone... You're using a CRM to stay organized with your job hunt, and you're also familiarizing yourself with the platform that your sales team will use when you land the job. This experience will only give you a competitive edge over other entry-level sales applicants.

If you're wondering what the most frequently used CRM is, it's (drumroll)...

Salesforce!

SALESFORCE.COM CRM

The #1 CRM used by the majority of sales teams today is Salesforce.com.

To get ahead and familiarize yourself with this tool before you even begin your job, I recommend you sign up and start using Salesforce right away.

You can get a Salesforce sales license for around $25, and it will provide you with the basics that you need to get a job in tech sales and make over $100,000 a year.

LINKEDIN PREMIUM OR SALES NAVIGATOR

In sales, your network is your net worth, and the only way to build and grow your network effectively on social media is by using LinkedIn every single day.

When you use LinkedIn every day to connect with new people, if you do not have an upgraded LinkedIn account the platform will limit you to viewing and messaging only a few profiles a day.

The best way to get around this is by investing in an upgraded LinkedIn Premium or Sales Navigator account.

LinkedIn Premium and Sales Navigator are both very similar. You essentially get unlimited searches with both and you can see who's viewed your profile as well (this can be a great networking opportunity).

However, with Sales Navigator, you get more advanced searching and filtering options, you can integrate your LinkedIn social media efforts with other tech tools you're using, and you get more opportunities to direct message (DM) hiring managers and recruiters you're not connected to yet via InMail (LinkedIn's direct messaging. When you have a basic account, you can only DM people you're already connected with).

You can sign up for a 30-day free trial of LinkedIn Sales Navigator and Premium. When you sign up and use the paid versions of LinkedIn for 30 days free you'll be able to see and connect with more people and grow your network faster. It's an absolute game-changer.

Once your free trial is up, depending on the package you choose, LinkedIn Premium ranges in price from $30 to $60 a month. And Sales Navigator can range in price from $80 and up per month, depending on what you select.

Check the prices for both, and if you can afford it, go with Sales Navigator because the search and outreach features they offer are unbeatable. But if the monthly expense is too high, go with LinkedIn Premium.

And at this stage in the book, since you already have a professional LinkedIn profile set up, now all you have to do is start connecting with the future sales leaders that would hire you and posting content about sales regularly. Don't overthink what you post. Think about the pains your followers are experiencing, and present solutions to those problems in your posts.

I will show you how to best use LinkedIn every day later on in this book. For now, make sure to sign up for an advanced version of this platform and start using it now.

ZOOM VIDEO

From interviews to meetings, a lot of events in the workspace are happening virtually these days rather than in person.

And out of all the video chat services on the market, Zoom Video is the #1 video communications and meeting platform in the world.

Nearly every sales team across the world uses it to execute remote video meetings with their company, customers, and prospects.

And nearly every hiring manager and recruiter uses Zoom to meet and interview job prospects.

Zoom is such an integral part of daily sales operations, no matter what level you are at a company, if you're serious about landing a job in tech sales, you need to learn how to use this platform fast.

Not only is Zoom free, but the best thing is it's foolproof to use. When you sign up, Zoom will walk you through all the important features you need to know to use it to its fullest potential.

As a word of warning, even though a good number of your job interviews and sales meetings (once you get the job) will take place on Zoom, this isn't an excuse to show up dressed casually. Follow our dress code rules in the marketing section and dress for the tech sales job you want to have. You should always dress professionally (at least from the waist up) and wear a dress shirt or blouse and even a jacket if you want.

Also, be sure to pick a place that is quiet with no visual distractions, has great lighting (you want the other person to be able to see you well), and is tidy.

In case you are taking interviews and meetings from a space you're insecure about (maybe you don't want the interviewer to see your messy dorm) you can always search Zoom video office background pictures. You can additionally search on Zoom for a background image to use or you can use WeWork (they have great office pictures as well). Whichever background you pick, just make sure it isn't flashy, inappropriate, or distracting. You want to be the star of the interview, not your background.

Once you sign up for Zoom and figure out what you want your background to look like, practice joining and hosting a few Zoom video meetings with your friends or family. Do some mock interviews with friends (we have a whole section on common sales interview questions, so stay tuned) and have them give an honest assessment of your performance. Sometimes body language and gestures we make in person can be distracting on video, so your friends can observe and look out for things like this.

By taking the time out to practice and get a hang of Zoom, when the time comes for you to log in for your official interview or meeting, you won't have any trouble showing up on time.

If you take these steps, you will impress the employer and give off the impression that you are not only on top of things, but you can accomplish anything and everything if they hire you.

CELL PHONE

To get and keep your dream job in tech sales, you are going to be on your cell phone A LOT.

You'll be talking to hiring managers, recruiters, gatekeepers (secretaries, assistants, etc.), and sales leaders about job opportunities.

And once you get the job, you'll consistently make prospecting calls, appointment-setting calls, and closing deals.

A cell phone is vital!

I assume you have a cell phone with unlimited talk, text, and internet data, but if you don't, you will want to get one ASAP.

There are plenty of cell phone carriers that will give you unlimited everything at reasonable prices.

Just search for a plan that fits within your budget, build a list with Seamless, and start dialing.

As far as what you should say when you get a hiring manager on the phone, keep reading because we cover plug-and-play scripts you can use to book meetings, schedule job interviews, and follow up.

GOOGLE GMAIL

Most companies use Google Workspace products as their primary technology.

For email, with approximately 1.5 billion people using Gmail across the globe, I can bet that this is your primary email provider.

The majority of sales professionals and HR people regularly use Gmail, so communication will be more efficient if you're both messaging from the same provider.

On top of that, with Gmail, there are countless organizational features that help you work smarter and build rapport more easily. You can save yourself time and schedule emails in advance. Plus with features like Smart Compose, Gmail will even help you draft your messaging.

Google Gmail has some of the most advanced features and functionalities for communicating with people in the world (I mean, it's the #1 email platform for a reason).

If you aren't already using Gmail, sign up for an account right now (it's free of course) and get into the habit of using it every day as your primary email provider.

GOOGLE CHROME

For web browsing, the #1 browser in the world, and the most advanced browser that tech salespeople use is Google Chrome.

Google Chrome makes web browsing and searching faster and easier.

Additionally, platforms like Seamless.AI and Salesforce have Chrome extensions that you can install to get the greatest use out of the tech tools you have and work from anywhere at any time.

For example, when you use the Chrome extension with Seamless.AI, you can pull up the website of a dream company you want to work for, and find the cell phones and emails of the sales leaders, HR, and anyone else you want to connect with.

If you aren't already using Chrome, download it today (again, it's free) and use it every day to make your job hunt easier.

CALENDAR APP

To land a solid tech sales job , or any good job for that matter, you have to not only make your schedule as open as possible, but you have to make it extremely easy for future employers to book an appointment with you.

If you make it difficult to get a time on the calendar to interview you (you're constantly going back and forth with the employer, trying to find a good time), then your chances of booking the interview and getting an offer are going to be extremely low. The employer is going to assume that you aren't worth the effort and the headache, and unfortunately move on to the next job candidate.

On the other hand, if you are a potential candidate who uses a Calendar app that makes scheduling an interview a no-brainer, you will drastically increase your chances of getting the interview and getting the job. And let me explain why...

Hiring managers and recruiters are incredibly busy people. So if you can make the job application process faster for them in any way, you're going to leave a lasting impression, and they're going to remember you in a positive light.

The best calendar tool I'd advise you to download is Calendly. Calendly will connect to your Google Workspace account and seamlessly sync with your calendar.

As you set up your Calendly account, you can input your preference for scheduling times. Maybe you anticipate that most of your interviews and meetings will only take 30 minutes or 60 minutes. You can indicate this with Calendly.

You can also indicate the time windows in the day when you are most available. For instance, I can do any 30 or 60-minute video interview from 8 AM to 12 PM. Calendly will take note of this.

Additionally, what's amazing about these scheduling tools like Calendly is, you just provide the HR person or the hiring manager with your link to your calendar in the scheduling app, and all they have to do is select a time slot to book an interview.

My entire sales team and HR team use Calendly to book hundreds of appointments a day with customers and job candidates.

Furthermore, when you use a tool like Calendly, you're gaining an edge over the competition because you're familiarizing yourself with platforms that many sales teams use. Even if a potential employer isn't using Calendly, I can guarantee they're using something similar. The fact that you have the gumption to learn how to use these platforms shows how proactive you are and it looks great on your resume.

Sign up for Calendly or a similar calendar scheduling tool, and put the calendar link in all of your email signatures, along with your name, your email, and your cell phone.

When you make it easy for people to interview and hire you... you make it easy to get a job in tech sales and make over $100,000 a year.

DIGITAL BUSINESS CARD

One of the fastest ways to impress a hiring team is to give them a digital business card.

A digital business card will include your name, title, company, cell phone, email, social media links, calendar scheduling tool, portfolio link, and any other important information that helps you separate yourself from the hundreds or thousands of applications recruiters sift through every day.

Digital business cards also have QR codes that you can save in your email signature and your text signature when you send messages to hiring managers or HR teams.

Whenever I meet with candidates who have digital business cards, I'm extremely impressed, and it makes my job of having to hire the best of the best candidates easier.

With a business QR code, we have all the information we need to quickly review a candidate and say "Yes" or "No" to interviewing them.

More than likely we will say yes to interviewing them because if I have to choose between Candidate A, where it takes an hour to look up and review their info, or Candidate B, where their info is readily available in an easy-to-review format, Candidate B is going to score the interview every time.

I guarantee you, as long as the information you provide on your digital business card is impressive (portfolio, resume, etc.), you're going to get the interview and the job.

Depending on how many cards you order, the price can vary from $20 to $150.

Here are some of my favorite business card creators that you can use to make your digital business card:

- www.blinq.me
- www.linktr.ee
- www.linqapp.com

PART 6

THE LISTS

Y ou are just one list away… from everything you want in life. The life you want, the family you want, the income you want, the houses you want, the vacations you want, the freedom you want… everything you want in this life is just one list away.

If you want to get a job in tech sales, you need to build a list of all the companies and contacts to sell yourself to.

Nothing gets sold to anyone without first building the list of people who desperately need what you have to offer, and then selling to everyone on the list.

If you can build the list and sell to the list, you will never be without work ever again in your lifetime.

In this section, I'm going to cover how to build your list, the tools that you need to automate all of your list-building, how to find contact info for anyone in seconds, and the secrets to make your list-building efforts seamless.

THE TWO LIST-BUILDING TOOLS YOU NEED

There are thousands of list-building platforms out there, but to save you the headache of testing out duds, you only need two technologies to build your prospecting list, and they are both free to use…

SEAMLESS.AI

If you don't have a list of contacts and their emails and cell phones, it's virtually impossible to get interviews with hiring managers.

That's where Seamless.AI comes in. It's a free list-building tool that is an absolute game-changer.

Seamless.AI finds cell phones, emails, and direct dials for anyone in seconds. My team and I built it so you can automate all your list-building work, manual CRM data entry work, and quit scouring millions of websites looking for contact info like emails and cell phones for sales leads.

With Seamless, you can build lists of hundreds of contacts and companies in seconds, get all their contact info instantly, and then automatically import all these lists into your favorite CRM or spreadsheet.

Artificial intelligence will magically research and verify their perfect emails and direct dials.

This platform additionally works on any website, on any social media profile, and even with your Gmail.

The best part of all… Seamless.AI is free to join and since you have this book I personally will give you $250 in free bonus credits for the platform when you write a book review.

Before Seamless, if you wanted to network with decision-makers or get a job at a top company, you had to go to the same country clubs or know the same people.

With Seamless, you eliminate all that extra work and instantly get the email addresses, cell phones, and direct dials to directly reach out to them with the click of a button.

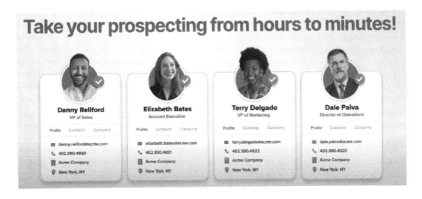

Use Seamless.AI to build your contact lists and company lists every day. Become an expert at using it to contact decision-makers at top companies you want to work for.

Join for free now at **www.seamless.ai** and check out a quick demo below:

bit.ly/seamlessAI

LINKEDIN

The next best platform to search for jobs, research companies, market yourself, and connect with HR people, VPs, directors, managers, etc. is LinkedIn.

LinkedIn will be great for company research, contact research, and relationship building. Unfortunately, it doesn't provide you with emails and phone numbers like Seamless does or allow you to export the data, but it is a great platform that salespeople use every day to network with their prospects.

Every day you should be using LinkedIn to learn about different companies and contacts that you want to work with. Throughout your job search, you should become a LinkedIn wizard. Connect with the hiring managers you find on LinkedIn, connect with the HR people you find on LinkedIn, and comment on everyone's posts, updates, etc.

You want to use these tools as much as possible to build meaningful relationships with the people that you want to work for.

Reach out and connect with contacts. Comment on their posts. And build rapport. This will help you book more interviews and get more job offers than anyone else.

* **Always personalize your connection request. This one is not personalized just for visual purposes.**

The most successful people that find a job in tech sales insanely fast are gurus at using Seamless.AI and LinkedIn every day.

Now that you have the top two list-building tools required for success, the next task is to build your company list.

COMPANY LIST: BUILD YOUR DREAM 100 LIST

To start building your lists to prospect for a job, you'll want to first create a company list which I call "The Dream 100."

The Dream 100 is where you build a list of all the top companies you would love to sell and work for.

The companies at the top of your list should be organizations you absolutely love. You should love the company culture, the product, the customers, the branding, and the target audience. All of it.

Some search criteria I would think about evaluating when building my company list are the following:

COMPANY INDUSTRY

Picking a company industry is a great place to start with building your dream 100 company list. First, think about what industry you want to work in and sell for.

For example, when I was in college, all I wanted to do was work in NYC for an adtech company (advertising technology) like Google, Yahoo, or IBM. When I was looking for tech sales jobs, I went after adtech companies and built my dream 100 around this industry.

People that work at Seamless.AI said they always wanted to sell sales technology and they fell in love with Seamless.AI and the sales tech space, etc.

Brainstorm and list out a few industries that you have some knowledge of, are passionate about, and could (with a high degree of confidence) sell for day in and day out. Once you have that list put these industries into Seamless or LinkedIn and start building your company list.

You can see hundreds of industries on Seamless and LinkedIn so just select the ones you like most.

COMPANY EMPLOYEE SIZE

Another one of my favorite company search filters when building my Dream 100 is using employee size.

Do you want to work for a small company or a big company? A small company will allow you to take on a lot of responsibilities, have a lot of ownership in starting and completing projects, minimal micro-management, oversight, etc. With a smaller company, you will have more freedom to create. You become a generalist and then the larger the company grows, the more you will need to become a specialist.

A large company will hire you to be a specialist in a very specific role that you work on day in and day out. You will have a lot of processes, systems, playbooks, and data all figured out. Getting started in your job at a larger company is much easier because you work on the same thing consistently trying to improve it.

For people with an entrepreneurial mindset, I would recommend smaller companies. For people who like structure and consistency, I would recommend bigger companies.

Employee sizes for companies typically range from 1-10, 11-50, 51-200, 201-500, 501-1000, 1001-5000, 5001-10,000, 10,000+. Pick the sizes that work best for you!

COMPANY LOCATION

Location could be a big factor in selecting the companies to put on your dream 100 list. For example, if you want to go into an office every day then you would want to select a company that is local in your area. Doing this would prohibit you from looking at companies in different locations. You might decide that you are more of an East Coast person and only want to work at East Coast HQ companies. You may love the hustle and bustle of Silicon Valley and only want to work for West Coast VC-backed companies. Leverage location as needed when building your Dream 100 list.

COMPANY KEYWORDS

The next search filter I love to use when building company lists is the keyword search filter in Seamless or LinkedIn.

When you are using the keyword search filter, you can type in any keyword and these platforms will show you all the companies that have that keyword in their profile.

For example, if you want to work for design software... you can input "design" in the keyword filter and "computer software" as the industry.

You will then get a list of all the computer software companies that have the word "design" somewhere on their company website or LinkedIn profile.

Using company keyword search filters is a great way to niche down on building your company lists.

COMPANY LIST-BUILDING CONCLUSION

Don't overthink building your dream 100 company list. I believe in **KISS: Keep It Stupid Simple**.

Select the search criteria that you think would be best for you, start building your dream 100 company list, and then it's time to quickly move on to building your contact lists of all the people who you should be prospecting to hire you.

I know we just went over a lot of different search filters and tools for building out your Dream 100 company list but I promise you – just get started – don't get overwhelmed.

CONTACT LISTS

Now that you've signed up for the two best list-building platforms, and you have the Dream 100 list of companies you want to work for, it's time to build your contact lists so you can start calling, emailing, social selling, and booking interviews with these companies. Let's talk about how to build your prospecting list and start getting in front of hiring managers for tech sales.

When prospecting for a job, you will need to sell yourself to two different groups of people.

The first group is called "HR."

These are all the people in Human Resources that manage the recruitment, hiring, and onboarding processes for a company.

HR people are essentially the gatekeepers who review all the candidates and decide who gets booked for an interview and who gets passed on. This is why it's critical to prospect them directly.

The second list that you will need to build will be the "Hiring Manager Titles." When you get that tech sales job, these are the people you will work with and/or report to.

You will want to build lists and execute prospecting campaigns for both lists to maximize your chances of getting interviews and breaking into your Dream 100 accounts.

Here are the HR titles you should build lists of and save in Seamless.AI and LinkedIn.

EXAMPLES OF HR TITLES

- Human Resources

- HR

- Recruiter

- Talent Acquisition

- Talent

- Hiring Manager

- Hiring

- People

- Human Resources Information System

- HRIS

- Benefits

- Employee

- Culture

- CHRO

- Chief Human Resources Officer

Whenever you have a company you're interested in, type in these different titles (along with the specific company) into the Seamless search engine and the LinkedIn search engine. You can also save these title searches into the platforms so you don't manually have to input them every time.

HIRING MANAGER TITLES

The next group of titles you need to build a list for are all the people who would hire you. These are the same people you will end up working for and reporting to should you get the job.

These include C-Suite, VPs, Directors, and Manager sales positions at the company (depending on company size).

You want to prospect the hiring managers because if a hiring manager tells HR to meet with you, you will skip the entire process and get an interview right away. That is the goal of targeting both hiring managers and HR managers.

EXAMPLES OF HIRING MANAGER TITLES

- VP Sales

- VP Business Development

- Chief Sales Officer

- Chief Revenue Officer

- Chief Executive Officer

- Chief Marketing Officer

- Director Sales

- Sales Director

- Director Business Operations

- Director, Sales Development

- Director, Inside Sales

- SDR Director

- Sales Ops

- Account Executives

- AEs

- SDR Manager

- Business Development Manager

- BDM

Build a list of every hiring manager and HR person at the companies that you want to work for.

Every day make sure that you reach out to contacts from both lists (HR Titles and Hiring Manager Titles).

And in case you're wondering if this process works, the candidates that build their lists and follow this approach book more interviews faster than anyone else.

In fact, some have even been hired within 24 - 48 hours of leveraging this approach.

But Brandon... That's A LOT of titles and contacts to go after!!

Yes, it is. If it were easy, everyone would do it. That being said, you've got the tools to do this insanely fast.

Save these search filters for both hiring managers and HR titles.

That way you can just add the company names to the searches, build your contact lists, then prep to launch your sales campaigns to these folks to book interviews.

Don't get overwhelmed if it's a lot of contacts or a little...

Just focus on getting the job done and done right.

If you want more interviews and job offers than ever before for the #1 profession in the world that lets you quit your shitty job, triple your income, work anywhere, and join the new rich…

I promise you it will be worth it.

Build the list and then it's time to sell to the list!

You may be asking yourself, *How many interviews do I need to book every day?*

Great question and it's pretty easy to answer by just using simple math.

Let's say that on average, out of all the companies you prospect, 10% turn into interviews. Then let's say your interviews convert to job offers at 20%.

If you built a list of 100 companies, that would convert to 10 interviews (100 companies x 10% = 10 job interviews) and 2 job offers (10 interviews x 20% = 2 job offers).

So if you're going after 20 companies a week and all the contacts at those companies… strive for a conversion rate of 10% and you will be booking anywhere from 2 - 4 interviews per week.

Don't forget, you need to reach out to multiple people at a company to break into an account and book interviews. If you're working with a 10% conversion rate, and you want to get the interview, remember that the more people you prospect, the better your chances are of getting in.

Now that you have your list-building strategy and the tools to get contact information, you'll need to figure out what to say when you get in front of these decision-makers. Talking to a hiring manager or human resources people can be intimidating if you are not prepared.

That is why in the next section I am going to give you everything you need to say and how to say it to book more interviews and generate more job offers!

In the next section, I will share with you all the scripts that you need to succeed.

Claim your FREE Bonus Bundle

HELP THOSE IN NEED

If this book helped you get started with your career in tech sales, can you help me out and take just 30 seconds right now to write an Amazon review: **www.amzn.to/3Yki4qT**

Your review will help shine a spotlight on this book so more people can see it, pick up a copy, and start their career in tech sales. The entire sales community benefits from you taking a minute to write a review. Isn't that incredible?

Plus, if you write an Amazon review, screenshot it, and upload it at **www.BrandonBornancin.com/techsalesbonus**, we will gift you this SICK bonus bundle, worth $1,935, but absolutely free for readers like you…

Scan to Write a Review & Claim Bonuses!

Total Value: $1,935

www.BrandonBornancin.com/techsalesbonus

PART 7

THE SCRIPTS

10-DAY PROSPECTING CAMPAIGN FOR INTERVIEWS

N ow that you have your lists, it's time to build your scripts.

Whenever you are about to prospect anyone for anything (a product, a service, or a job) you need to plan out your prospecting campaigns in advance.

When I say plan out your prospecting campaign in advance, I mean you are going to plan out how many calls, voicemails, emails, text messages, video messages, etc. you're going to send out across a specific number of days.

I know what you're thinking, *Why can't I just let whatever happens happen?* Or, *Why can't I just reach out until I get a response*?

But you never want to randomly reach out because it's like shooting from the hip. And shooting from the hip with no strategy is like getting in your car and setting out to drive from Ohio to California without a map. If you don't have a concrete plan, you'll never reach your destination, and you'll end up wasting time, energy, and gas money.

So you always want to have a plan, and a campaign is your greatest chance at success.

To prospect for interviews at your dream jobs, I recommend using a 10-day prospecting campaign across two full weeks. This is because a one-week campaign is too short, and anything over 10 days will be overkill.

Ten days is a good sweet spot because if people aren't getting back to you within that time frame, then there likely isn't a sales job opportunity there at this time.

In this book we will first plan the calendar and create the campaign, then we will write the scripts.

Below is a 10-day prospecting campaign model with 17 sales touches (a sales touch is any kind of contact with a prospect. It could be a call, an email, a voicemail, etc.) to book a sales job interview.

Channel	Emails	Calls	Voicemails	LinkedIn	Video
Day 1	Em 1	Call 1	Vm 1		
Day 2	Em 2			LI Connection Request	
Day 3		Call 2			Vid 1
Day 4			Vm 2		
Day 5	Em 3				
Day 6		Call 3			Vid 2
Day 7			Vm 3	LI Msg 2	
Day 8	Em 4				
Day 9		Call 4			
Day 10			Vm 4	LI Msg 3	

Try not to phone it in and skip this step. Seventeen sales touches may sound like a lot of hard work, but you honestly have to toughen up. Gaining financial freedom is hard, but being poor is even harder. So choose your hard, and remember – to maximize your success, you have to put in the dedication.

Secondly, when you launch this prospecting campaign you'll have great practice for the real thing because this campaign is very similar to the sales campaigns you'll execute every day at work when you start your tech job.

Ultimately, your goal with these campaigns is to book a job interview. So with every touch, you're essentially pitching the prospective employer on giving you the chance to work for them full-time.

In the next sections, we will give you plug-and-play scripts to use for the touch points in this 10-day campaign.

SCRIPTS

Once you get the contact information of a hiring manager or a recruiter, you'll need a fire script that sells them on the talent, passion, and hunger you can bring to a tech sales position at their company.

I've got hundreds of scripts, templates, and strategies for each channel you need to write for:

- Cold calls

- Cold emails

- LinkedIn connection requests

- LinkedIn messages

- Custom video messages

- Etc.

However, if I explained them all to you in this book, you would have a thousand-page book in your hands. And no one has the time to sift through that much information, especially when getting into tech sales is all about action.

Instead, to keep things as simple as possible, in this section I give you sample scripts and frameworks that you can use for each channel.

Some scripts are broader, while others are tailored to Seamless (as if you were reaching out to prospect for a job at Seamless). However broad or narrow, every script does an excellent job of…

#1) Demonstrating to the HR contact that you did your research on them and the company.

#2) Enticing them with a specific value proposition that you can bring to their organization.

#3) Closing with a specific call to action (CTA).

You want to follow this formula of Demonstrating - Enticing - Closing with every touch point.

Keep in mind that we don't offer up a script for every single touch point in your 10-day campaign. If I were to give you a script for every touch, you wouldn't learn how to write your own messaging, which is an invaluable skill if you want to thrive in tech sales.

So take the scripts I provide for you, personalize them, make them your own, and use them as inspiration to write the remainder of the scripts you need for your campaign.

And if you would like additional scripts and templates for specific channels, I've included these materials in the all-access bonuses that you get when you write a book review on Amazon and send your screenshot to:

www.BrandonBornancin.com/techsalesbonus

CHOOSE ONLY ONE CALL TO ACTION

As I mentioned in the previous section, with every script you want to demonstrate, entice, and close with a specific call to action (CTA).

Before I give you script ideas, I wanted to take a minute to cover the

CTA step because it's so important in determining your success with prospecting.

A call to action is a request you make for someone to do something and take some kind of action. A call to action is the element that gives your messaging some forward momentum. Without a call to action, your message will fall flat and end up in the trash.

A lot of times people who are new to sales make the mistake of throwing out several different CTAs. But when you are prospecting a potential employer for a job, make sure you use only ONE CTA.

When I coach students in our sales masterminds about using only one CTA, I use the following analogy:

Let's say you're stranded in the middle of nowhere, and you haven't eaten for a week. You look across the field, and to your amazement, you see three rabbits.

What's your best move?

Is it to catch all three rabbits?

Or is it to just catch one?

Well, if you try to catch all three rabbits at once, guess what happens?

You end up catching no rabbits because they all see your movement, they figure out that you're trying to hunt them, and they scurry away, leaving you to starve to death.

However, if you try to catch only one rabbit, you dramatically increase your chances of capturing it, eating it, and surviving.

Try to catch all three, and you perish.

Focus all your efforts on one, and you survive and thrive.

The same is true with calls to action.

If people reading your emails see multiple CTAs – for example, you ask them to call you back, send you more information, book an interview, and hire you – all these CTAs are going to confuse them and they're going to delete your message, or hang up the phone.

So instead of dropping multiple CTAs, drop one.

During the prospecting stages, you could simply ask them to call you back or send you info about what they're looking for in a sales rep or what their application process is like. You could also ask them to book a quick call with you to discuss their sales position. If you've already interviewed with the hiring manager, you could ask for an offer or an update on the status of your application. Whatever stage you are at in the job process, only drop one call to action. And regardless of the specific CTA that you make, be sure that you inject urgency into your request.

Tell them to get back to you at their earliest convenience with a "Yes" or "No" because you have a lot of opportunities on the table. Even if you have ZERO job offers, don't be afraid to apply some pressure and make the employer realize all the value that's in front of them. This will help to speed up the process and get you closer to signing an offer.

Whether we're talking about calls, emails, voicemails, or video messages – whatever the medium is – make sure you squeeze the urgency out of the situation and only make one call to action.

SAMPLE COLD CALL SCRIPTS

COLD CALL 1:

Hi {{first_name}} – Happy {{day of the week}}!

I'm a huge fan! Congrats on the new round of funding and product features you just released.

The software you deliver for companies like X & Y is changing the industry.

Can I get 27 seconds real quick?

Awesome!

I'm reaching out because I noticed you are building out your sales team, and looking to hire new SDRs.

I'm all in on starting a career in tech sales.

I've been studying the best software sales experts and I know how to do whatever it takes to execute a predictable and repeatable sales systems to generate millions in pipeline and sales.

I'd love to schedule an interview to meet with you and share the results I can drive to fill the calendar with qualified appointments and demos.

Do you have any time right now or does tomorrow work best for a quick interview chat?

COLD CALL 2:

Hi {{first_name}} – This is {{your_name}}, love what you're doing at company X! Huge fan!

Do you have 17 seconds?

Awesome!

I started following Brandon on LinkedIn, and I saw that you're expanding your sales team.

I just wanted to see if we could pencil in time for an SDR interview.

With my experience at {{past job}} and passion, I am beyond ready to max my potential and begin my career in sales with Seamless.

The world should be prospecting with Seamless!

Do you have some time later this week so we could meet up to discuss this?

SAMPLE VOICEMAIL SCRIPTS

VOICEMAIL 1:

Hello {{first_name}} – This is {{your_name}}. Huge fan of Seamless.AI!

I'm calling because with {{achievement 1}} I have the skills and the track record of crushing goals to help your sales team at Seamless. AI improve {{results}}.

I wanted to see if we could have a quick conversation about how I can help your sales team scale their results.

I can be reached at {{sender.phone_number}}.

Again, that's {{sender.phone_number}}.

Give me a call. We're wasting time.

Thanks!

VOICEMAIL 2:

Hi {{first_name}} – This is {{your_name}}. Love everything you're doing at Seamless!

I {{sent an email/ left a message}} at the start of the week regarding sales job postings at Seamless.AI and thought I'd see if now was a good time to reach out again.

Just to reiterate, I have driven M results at {{past experience 1}} and I'd love to discuss how I can help your sales team generate {{result}}.

Call me back so I can share more.

My number is: {{sender.phone_number}}.

Again, that's {{sender.phone_number}}.

Thanks so much! Looking forward to hearing from you.

VOICEMAIL 3:

Hi {{first_name}} – My name is {{your_name}}. You're doing big things at Seamless.

And I'm calling to see how I can contribute towards your mission to $100M and IPO.

I sincerely think {{soft skill 1}} sets me apart from others and can make a huge difference for your sales team who are looking to {{goal}}.

If you're interested in learning more about what I can bring to the table, give me a call back.

My number is: {{sender.phone_number}}.

Again that's {{sender.phone_number}}.

Thanks so much! Looking forward to hearing from you.

SAMPLE COLD EMAIL SCRIPTS

SUBJECT LINE OPTIONS

- {{mutual contact}} suggested I reach out

- {{first_name}}, I saw you're focused on {{goal}}

- Let me help your sales team reach {{goal}}

- Can I help?

- Talk on {{day}} at {{time}}

- Tired of salespeople who never give up?

- Need help with X?

- Quick question

- We met at {{event}}

- I have an idea for {{sales team goal}}

- We have X in common

- Contacting you at REFERRAL'S suggestion

- REFERRAL NAME

- Who is in charge of sales at company X?

- {{your_name}}

- {{your_name/company X}}

- Quick request

- Trying to connect

- {{company X}}

- {{your_name}} – {{desired job title}}

- Thank you, {{first_name}}

COLD EMAIL 1: INTRO

Hey Brandon – Congrats on all your success with Seamless.AI!

I recently picked up your book, *Whatever It Takes,* and I'm excited to take my sales skills to the next level.

I'm reaching out because I would love to work for Seamless.AI!

I saw that you are hiring hundreds of SDRs, and I promise you, if I joined the team, I'd be your top performer, booking hundreds of appointments every month!

I want a lifelong career in sales, and there's no better place to become the best salesperson than at Seamless.AI.

Are you the best person to speak with about interviewing for your SDR job or is there someone you can refer me to?

Thank you!

My best,
{{your_name}}
{{your_email}}
{{your_cell number}}

COLD EMAIL 2: FOLLOW-UP

Hey {{first_name}}! Friendly follow-up.

Thank you again for taking the time out to talk with me. I really appreciate it.

I am so pumped and looking forward to getting the chance to help your sales team reach {{goal}}.

I wanted to keep the ball rolling. If you don't mind me asking, what are the next steps in the process?

My best,
{{your_name}}
{{your_email}}
{{your_cell number}}

COLD EMAIL 3: REFERRAL

Hey {{first_name}}!

I heard about your latest {{achievement}}, and glad to see you doing so well! I'm a HUGE fan!

I have a quick favor to ask.

Would you mind providing an intro for me to {{referral name}}?

I noticed you two are connected and I'd love to chat with them about how I could contribute {{hard skill 1}} and {{soft skill 1}} to helping the sales team scale their efforts.

I am all in on spreading the word about the #1 sales software so an intro would help me out a ton.

Talk soon!

{{your_name}}
{{your_email}}
{{your_cell number}}

SAMPLE LINKEDIN MESSAGES

LI MESSAGE 1: CONNECTION REQUEST COLD

Hi {{first_name}} – I am a big fan of all the amazing things you're doing at Seamless! And I love connecting with game-changing {{recipient role}} like you.

I stumbled across your profile, and we actually have a lot in common like {{shared traits, experience, etc}}.

I'd love to become a valuable connection for you and share how my time at {{past job position}} could help Seamless on your journey from {{point a}} to $100M and IPO.

Let's connect and talk all things Seamless.

All the Best,
{{your_name}}

LI MESSAGE 2:

Hey Brandon, I built a list of 100 companies in software that desperately need Seamless.AI.

I am so motivated and eager to fill your sales team's calendars with back-to-back appointments.

Can we pencil in 10 minutes for a quick SDR job interview?

You let me know what time works best, and I will be sure to accommodate.

Best,
{{your_name}}

LI MESSAGE 3: REFERRAL REQUEST

Hey {{first_name}}

I loved your latest post on {{topic}}. It was a totally different perspective that I hadn't considered before.

Quick ask… Would you mind providing an intro for me to {{referral name}}?

I noticed you are connected to {{referral name}} and I'd love to chat with them about where they see the sales team at Seamless going in the next year and how I can be an immediate asset to you guys.

I'm looking to {{professional growth goal}} and this would help me a ton!

Regards,
{{your_name}}

SAMPLE INTERVIEW FOLLOW-UP SCRIPTS

SUBJECT LINE OPTIONS

- Thank you, {{first_name}}

- Appreciate your time!

- It was a pleasure meeting with you!

- Thank you for your time!

- Thank you – {{your_name}}, {{job title}}

INTERVIEW FOLLOW-UP 1:

Hello Brandon,

It was great meeting you and the entire team for the SDR job interview.

The energy, the integrity, and the intelligence of everyone is better than any company I ever interviewed for.

I can't wait to help put Seamless in the hands of every single salesperson who desperately needs it (which is all of them!).

I'm eager to master all your training, work harder than everyone else every day, crush the dialer, crush prospecting, and help the company make millions.

What are the best next steps to getting an offer and finalizing the opportunity to join the team?

Best,
{{your_name}}

INTERVIEW FOLLOW-UP 2:

Hi Brandon, Happy {{day of the week}} and congrats on the results you've been delivering for {{mention 2 or 3 clients from President's Club website}}.

Because I'm eager to help you win all the companies and customers in your market, I noticed DocuSign is a customer...

And one of the fastest ways to book new appointments and close new customers is with look-alike customer lists.

Since you already work with DocuSign, have you thought about selling to:

- Adobe Echosign

- PandaDoc

- HelloSign

- SignNow

- EverSign

- DocHub

- Proposify

- RightSignature

- Etc.

I'd love to get to work booking qualified demos and appointments with these companies.

What are the best next steps to get an offer and get started?

Please let me know.

I'm all in on taking Seamless to every sales team in the world.

All the Best,
{{your_name}}

INTERVIEW FOLLOW-UP 3:

Hi Brandon,

Happy {{day}}!

I've been writing scripts and researching companies to prospect. And I've been practicing my elevator pitch, so if given the opportunity to join your company as your next top SDR... I will hit the ground running.

I'm hard-working, humble, positive, coachable, and I will do whatever it takes to learn your sales systems, playbooks, processes, and scripts.

If you have any questions or concerns, I'd be happy to jump on a call to address them.

What are the best next steps to review your job offer and hit the ground running?

Regards,
{{your_name}}

INTERVIEW FOLLOW-UP 4:

Hey {{first_name}},

I wanted to thank you for meeting with me {{day}} to discuss the sales rep position at Seamless.AI.

I am striving to become the best salesperson I can be. So it only makes sense to work for the best sales software company out there!

Unlike other candidates, with my {{hard skill 1}}, {{soft skill 1}}, and {{achievement 1}}, I will bring ownership and that relentless WIT attitude to the position that's sorely missing in tech sales today.

What are the best next steps to get an offer and hit the ground running? I'm trying to make an impact at this company NOW!

Cheers,
{{your_name}}

PART 8

THE ACTIVITY

I n order to book as many job interviews and get as many offers as possible, you need to put in the sales activity.

In this section, I am going to teach you all the sales activity you need to execute and track daily to get the job in tech sales that you want insanely fast.

Before I get started, I want to shatter the biggest myth and misconception of them all related to job searching…

THE WORST WAY TO GET A JOB IN TECH SALES

Do you want to know the worst way to get a job in tech sales?

It's going to a job site and just submitting your resume. Then sitting and waiting for the phone to ring.

You heard me right. It's going to a job app site, sending in your resume, and praying and hoping that you land your dream job.

How many resumes do you think I've reviewed?

Just take a guess…

How many resumes do you think a busy CEO reads with 500 employees, over 300,000 customers, and millions of followers at one of the top software companies in the world?

Are you ready?

ZERO.

That's right. I've never reviewed a single resume that was submitted by a candidate.

Now that doesn't mean that resumes aren't important, because Human Resources (HR) and hiring managers will require them just to put you into the HR systems.

However, to be transparent with you, the real reason they require you to submit a resume is for organizational reasons, so they can have your name on a list in a CRM of potential candidates.

So if resumes are only needed for organizational reasons, hoping that this piece of paper gets you your dream tech sales job is just plain foolish.

More importantly, just submitting a resume is a terrible strategy because you aren't doing anything to make an impression or stand out to the decision-makers and the sales team who would hire you.

Submitting a resume and doing nothing else is like having an important test and doing nothing to prepare for it. No studying, no research, and no hard work to make sure you ace the test.

We all know if you have a life-changing test coming up, to ace it, you need to take massive action to increase your odds of getting the best grade possible. You have to read the chapters in the book over and over again. Create flashcards. Participate in study groups. Take practice tests. It's a lot of work, but with every action you take, you get closer to getting an A+ on the test.

Getting a job in tech sales is no different. The only way to win at tech sales, and anything in life, is by doing more activity than anyone else. The more activity you execute, the greater your chances are of winning.

Action is the move that sets you apart from all the other players on the field.

Activity is the name of the game when you are trying to get a tech sales job.

The majority of the people I've hired took massive action to get their jobs. They prospected me via cold calling, emailing, social media, video messages, texts, you name it. They went all out to sell me and show me why they would be the best person to add to our sales team. The majority of the salespeople we've ever hired (and we've hired over 1,000 people since launching the company) prospected every single person on the sales team and showed us why we needed to hire them right away.

The salespeople who get jobs in tech sales always go above and beyond just submitting their resume and hoping things work out. They reach out to every decision-maker on the team. They prospect every influencer and pitch us on how they will transform sales, help us book more appointments, close more deals, and increase the company's brand awareness. They essentially sell us on why we should hire them. And they do whatever it takes to show us why they are the best person for the job.

If you doubt how effective it is to take the extra step and reach out like this, I promise you – it works! The people who do this type of activity are the people who get hired in tech sales!

If you want to get a job in tech sales as fast as humanly possible, don't just submit your resume and wish for the best.

You want to prospect and sell every single decision-maker, influencer, and team member at the company who might interview you and hire you.

Now that I've shared the importance of doing the maximum activity to get the offer, I'm going to show you the daily activity you need to execute to cut through the noise, book interviews, and get the job.

TRACKING YOUR METRICS

To get that dream job in tech sales fast, you need to track the following activity metrics every single day...

LEADS

A lead is a contact at a company that you need to reach out to for a job interview.

A lead can be a hiring manager, HR, talent acquisition, VP, director, manager, etc. A lead can be anyone in this Inner Circle, from HR to the sales team, who's in charge of filling your position.

Depending on how fast you want to get hired, you will want to reach out to 10 - 100 leads per day.

Keep in mind here that sometimes you may end up having to reach 30 people (that's 30 leads) at a single company to get that tech sales job, so that can be a full day's worth of lead generation.

More importantly, the more leads you research to sell to, the greater your chances of success. When I was job searching back in the day, I set big goals for myself, and I would reach out to 100 leads a day. Unfortunately back then I didn't have tools like Seamless.AI that could give me their emails and cell phones instantly in seconds, so I wasted a lot of time on list-building.

Luckily for you, you don't have to waste your precious time. Instead, use Seamless.AI and LinkedIn, build your contact list, and get to work executing your sales campaigns!

CALLS

Track all the calls you make to leads in a spreadsheet.

I would recommend trying to make up to 4 calls per lead over two sales weeks (10 days).

And shoot for a 5 to 20% conversion rate.

EMAILS

You will want to track all of the emails that you send to hiring managers and sales leads.

You should send out up to 4 emails per lead over two sales weeks (10 days).

Shoot for a 5 to 20% conversion rate.

SOCIAL

You should send out three LinkedIn messages per lead (with the first being a connection request) over two sales weeks (10 days).

Shoot for a 5 to 20% conversion rate.

VIDEO

You can also test out custom videos. I've hired quite a few people who sent videos, pitching me on why they'd be a great addition to the team.

I wouldn't send more than 1 - 2 videos to a prospect if you decide to try this channel.

LEVERAGE DIFFERENT CHANNELS

Always try different channels in order to book that interview. Different personas use different sales channels. Some will respond to calls. Some will respond to emails. Some will respond to social media engagement. And some will like videos. Always try different channels in order to book that interview.

INTERVIEWS

Next, you need to track the number of interviews you attend. This will help you understand your leads-to-interview conversion rates and your interviews-to-job offer conversion rates.

Depending on the number of leads you contact a day, and how aggressive you want to be, you'll want to try to book anywhere between 3 to 10 interviews a week.

If you convert those interviews at 20% conservatively, you will generate 2 job offers for every 10 interviews you go on!

By leveraging the strategies and secrets in this book you can get as high as 50% interview-to-job offer (in other words, half of the interviews you go on can turn into job offers if you leverage the secrets I share with you).

JOB OFFERS

The last activity metric you will want to track is job offers.

Job offers are employment agreements decision-makers put together for you to join their company.

Your ultimate goal should be to get as many job offers as possible with your dream tech sales companies so you can figure out which organization is best for you to maximize your success.

The job offer is the ultimate metric all your hard work is leading up to. If you are putting in the activity and tracking your metrics daily… The job offers will roll in!

PROSPECTING IS NOT ONE-SIZE-FITS-ALL

Prospecting for interviews and job offers is never a one-size-fits-all approach. This is why you need to leverage all the sales channels available to you.

The more contacts you make with the leads you research, the more interviews you will book, and the more offers you will receive.

Remember the sales funnel we walked you through earlier in the book?

The more leads you research and sell to, the more interviews you will book.

The more interviews you attend, the more job offers you will get.

This means the more activity you do at the top of the job search funnel, the more offers you will get at the bottom of the funnel.

Do whatever it takes to maximize the sales activity you execute every day to get a job in tech sales.

Pay attention to these metrics and track them daily because they will let you know how you are doing and what you need to train on.

If you find that your activity is low for any key metric then work on increasing it. Increase your calls, your emails, and your social touches.

If you find that you're not booking as many interviews as you should, work on improving your messaging, your pitching, and the value you pitch to the employer.

If you find you aren't getting as many offers as you should, practice your elevator pitch, interviewing Q&A, objection handling, closing, and work on your follow-up scripts.

If any metrics are trending down, review them and diagnose them like a doctor.

THE ACTIVITY FUNNEL

Now let's take these metrics and turn them into a funnel. In sales, a funnel visually shows you the journey a customer takes from initially becoming aware of your product to deciding to buy.

In your case, your funnel will show the journey you want the company to take from first encountering your messaging (via email, call, etc.) to deciding that you're the perfect candidate, and making an offer.

THE LEADS / AWARENESS STAGE

Once you generate leads, you begin the Awareness Stage where you send out LinkedIn connection requests, emails, and calls, make introductions and put yourself on the radar of key people at the companies you're interested in.

As the stage name indicates, this is the part in the funnel where you want to make these companies "aware" of you – that you exist, and you are quality talent they should look into.

Many leads are going to pass on you. That's why it's the biggest part of the funnel! But others are going to continue the conversation, and see what you're all about.

Your goal during this stage is to be consistent with your communication (reach out via social, call, email) and your follow-ups.

You want to show the leads the value you bring to the table through your resume, relevant experience, skills, results you've delivered at jobs in the past, your goals for the future, etc.

The ultimate goal at the leads stage is to book the interview.

THE INTERVIEW STAGE

The Interview Stage is where those leads who are interested in working with you book an interview to meet with you. They are going to meet you in person or virtually and ask you all the questions we will cover in the next section of this book (so keep reading for that).

Your goal at this stage is to crush the interview and move on to the Job Offer Stage.

The best way to do this is to master the interview section of this book and study everything we cover.

THE JOB OFFER STAGE

The final stage in the funnel is getting a job offer. This is where the company decides they want to hire you.

If a company decides that they don't want to extend you an offer, reach out and see why they didn't hire you. You can use this information to improve your approach with future job opportunities. And please keep in touch. You never know – circumstances may change at a company, and if they do – you will be at the top of their mind.

Just like with sales campaigns, with your activity metrics, you always want to work to improve your conversion rates.

If out of 100 leads, you're booking 10 interviews (that's a 10% conversion rate by the way), that number could always be better!

So constantly work on your conversion rates to get hired by increasing your activity.

Increase the lists you build, the leads you research, the calls you make, the emails you send, and the people you connect with on social media.

WAYS TO IMPROVE SALES FUNNEL METRICS

I frequently get asked, "How do I improve my conversion rates for the different stages of the funnel? How do I book more interviews and turn more interviews into offers?"

I am going to break down 4 key pillars you should work on improving every day to increase your conversion rates at each stage of the funnel. I call these key pillars, **LSTA**:

- **Lists:** Use Seamless.AI or LinkedIn (or both) to build the list of contacts and companies every day and go after the list.

  You can build more niche lists in specific niches and industries to get job offers… or you can just increase the amount of leads that you research in a list.

  Both will help increase your chances of getting more interviews and job offers.

  Always remember that you are just one list away from the dream tech sales job you want and the dream life you want.

- **Scripts:** Create a Google doc and re-write the scripts that we give you in *The Ultimate Guide To Breaking Into Tech Sales*. Study your scripts, memorize them, test them every single day, and optimize them to make them your own. Try to improve your scripts and performance every day to maximize conversion rates from leads to interviews, and interviews to offers.

- **Training:** Every day you want to train to improve these metrics. Re-read this book, practice your interviewing skills, and practice your email, social, and text cadences every day.

- **Activity:** Every day increase your activity (studying, research, etc.) by 1% and increase your winning mindset behavior (embracing change, doing more with less, etc.) by 1%.

ACTION BEATS INACTION EVERY TIME

One of the principles that I live by is to improve 1% every day no matter what.

This is a principle I teach my entire company. If you improve 1% every day, by the end of a calendar year, you'll improve 37x. This means if you start the year making $100,000... and you improve by just 1% every day... By the end of the year, you will be making over $3,700,000.

Isn't that insane?

This is why Warren Buffet says compounding interest is the 8th wonder of the world! It's so powerful and one of the quickest tools to leverage to become financially free.

Improving 1% every day is like building a bridge.

No one can build a bridge overnight.

But if you consistently work at it, brick by brick, your daily hard work will result in a big beautiful bridge in no time. I believe the bridge you slowly work on bit by bit is taking you from Point A (your biggest problems, challenges, and struggles in life) to Point B (your greatest goals, dreams, and desires).

Putting in the activity to improve 1% a day will help you build your bridge to success.

Every single day, if you work at building prospecting lists, selling to the lists, booking more appointments, reaching out to hiring managers, cold calling, emailing, and social selling VPs, directors – the Inner Circle – all this work you put in daily will produce massive returns!

Remember, practice doesn't just make perfect, but it gives you the confidence and the momentum to get the job.

Know your sales funnel in order to get your dream job in tech sales.

And never forget that what gets measured gets improved and done. What doesn't get measured, doesn't get done.

When you put in the activity, the activity will work for you and produce more leads, interviews, and job offers.

Good luck!

PART 9

THE INTERVIEW

N ow that you've executed your 10-day prospecting campaign and scored some interviews before the big day comes, you want to do lots of R-E-S-E-A-R-C-H.

You want to invest a lot of time into learning everything you can about the company.

The most competitive sales job candidates are those who know everything about the company and showcase this knowledge in their interviews. They show how well they can sell the company and they highlight how positive, coachable, hard-working, and hungry they are to hit the ground running with their position.

A couple days before your interview, create a Google doc or sheet, and start answering the following questions to ensure that you're prepared for anything the HR team throws your way:

- What does the company sell?

- Who are the company's customers? Expert tip: Customers are typically highlighted on the homepage or case studies section of a website.

- What industry is the company in? What markets does the company serve?

- What are the problems that the company solves?

- What is the business model of the company? How do they make money?

- What is the pricing of the products?

- Who are the competitors?

- Why do you think the company you are interviewing with is better than the competition?

- Who is on the team (the C-Suite, VPs, Directors, Managers, etc.)?

- What is the employee count?

- When was the company founded?

- What is the history of the company?

- What products do they sell?

- What can you learn from the company's advertising and marketing? How do they position themselves in the market?

- What is the mission and vision of the company?

- What can you learn about the culture from their social media feed?

- What are some case studies (you want to memorize a couple of case studies – I'm talking names, results, and success stories with the company here)?

You'll want to go through this process and answer each of these questions for every interview you have with a new company.

Yes, this will take 1 - 4 hours of research to do but trust me, it's worth it.

Most candidates come into an interview unprepared and they typically try to wing it. So there's nothing more impressive to a hiring manager than a candidate who knows the company and takes the time out to do their homework.

Personally speaking, my team and I will never hire someone who knows absolutely nothing about our company, our products, our people, our mission, or our customers.

Additionally, you will get much faster every time you complete interview pitch prep for a company. So this work will get easier over time.

Here are some sites that will help you collect this interview meeting prep Q&A as fast as possible:

SEAMLESS.AI

Seamless will give you all the contact information, pitch intelligence, social media info, and data like growth rate, revenue, and industry.

Seamless is an absolute gold mine that many people interviewing for their first job in tech sales don't even know about.

Use Seamless to research the company, the HR team, and the leadership team.

THE COMPANY WEBSITE

The company website, specifically the "About" page and the homepage are treasure troves of information about what the company does, customer logos (brands that are clients of the company), industry info, you name it.

The homepage will also include links to social media profiles you can review. Leverage the website to answer as many interview prep questions as possible.

LINKEDIN

There is so much interview prep research you can do on LinkedIn.

Visit the company's LI profile and the individual profiles of leadership and HR to find out about the latest company news (awards, product releases, press releases, etc.) as well as goals and initiatives.

Also use LinkedIn to review the background of the HR team, leadership, and the person who is interviewing you (if you're given a name in advance). This way if anyone asks you a question about anything in the interview, you are ready to roll!

GOOGLE

Google can be one of your best friends when doing company and contact research. Go ahead and put the company into the Google search engine along with the individual contact names you want to research. You will learn all types of good information this way.

WIKIPEDIA

If the organization you're applying to is a mid-market or enterprise company (500 employees and up), they'll likely have a Wikipedia page. Wikipedia can offer incredibly rich intelligence about a company, especially the origin story and the company's standing in the market. Wikipedia unfortunately won't be an option if you're trying to work for a startup. But maybe that will change in the future with your help!

In addition to these outlets, if the company has their own books, white papers, podcasts, or course training, check those all out as well.

Once you put in the grunt work and find the answers to these questions, study, memorize them, and you will be prepared to ace your interview.

CRUSHING YOUR INTERVIEW QUESTIONS

In sales, you have to prepare for objections (excuses a prospect gives for why they can't buy your solution) and questions before you pitch a prospect.

Preparing for sales objections is just like being a pro athlete and studying the defense of the opposing team. When you know what questions, concerns, and objections to expect and how to address them, you demonstrate your credibility to the prospect. You get them to realize that you have the best solution on the market (i.e. your skills and talent), and you close them.

You can use this same strategy to ace your interview.

Before you ever meet for an interview, you should brainstorm every possible question a hiring manager or recruiter may ask you, and prepare your answers in advance.

You want to treat the interview like it's a test and not only prepare your own answer key, but memorize your answers so when the interview day arrives, you won't be nervous. You'll instead be calm, prepared, and better able to focus on building rapport with the interviewer.

To prepare you for your big tech sales interview, we came up with some of the most common questions you're bound to hear in an entry-level job interview. Read through these questions, prepare your answers, and add them to a Google doc. Once you have your Google doc, memorize your answers and role-play with your family and friends.

As you go on your interviews, take note of the responses that impress hiring managers, and the answers that fall flat, and constantly improve.

Lastly, remember this: A job interview is like a sale.

Your aim is to sell the interviewer on YOU.

You want to convince them that you are the PERFECT person for the job.

So frame every answer around what YOU can do for THEM.

Here are some interview questions, to prepare to answer, in no particular order.

As a disclaimer, if you're reading *The Ultimate Guide To Breaking Into Tech Sales*, and have ZERO sales experience, no worries. Skip any sales-specific questions.

And if you have some sales experience, make sure you answer those questions first:

- When was your Start and End Date in your last role? Why did you choose to join your last company?

- What were your goals, KPIs, and responsibilities for this role?

- What results did you deliver at your last job? How did you achieve those results?

- What is your experience with high-volume sales activity (sales calls / emails / social touches / meetings / deals)?

- What was the team size at your previous job? How was it structured and organized?

- What tech stack did your team use? What did you like or dislike about it?

- We get 1,000 applications a month. Why are you the best person for the job out of the 1,000 people who applied?

- Why are you looking to move on from your current job?

- What did you enjoy the most about your previous job? And what did you enjoy the least?

- What were your biggest challenges at your last job? How did you overcome them?

- If we get to the reference stage, what should I expect to hear when I speak with your manager?

- What was your manager's style? What did you like about working with them? What did you dislike about working with them? What did you like and dislike about your team?

- What are you looking for in your next job?

- Why do you want a career in sales?

- How did you perform against your peers if you had to stack rank?

- How did you learn how to sell?

- What sales experience do you have (if any)?

- What is your daily routine?

- What is your favorite sales book?

- Who is your favorite sales influencer or thought leader?

- What type of work environment do you thrive in?

- Cold call me and I am going to be the prospect. Sell me your favorite product. Go ahead and pick up the virtual phone and give me a ring right now. Start by saying "Ring! Ring!"

- How would you pitch me our products and services if I was a prospect and we were in a meeting right now?

- Write a sample cold email as if you were selling for us, and send it to me in five minutes. The clock starts now.

- What struggles have you faced in your life, and what did you do to overcome them?

- How much money do you wanna make?

- Tell me about a time you were given feedback or coaching advice and how did you implement it?

Once you prepare your answers to these questions, get ready to close every prospective employer that you interview with!

WIIFTE:
WHAT'S IN IT FOR THE EMPLOYER?

When you are going in for an interview, one of the most important factors you want to focus on is WIIFTE: What's In It For The Employer?

You want to make your pitch all about what's in it for the employer and how they would benefit if they hire you out of the thousands of candidates who applied to the position.

How are you going to bring value?

Why are you the best person possible to maximize the success of the company?

These are the questions you want to come up with answers for to cut through the noise because the majority of candidates go into an interview focused on what the company can do for them.

But the top candidates show selflessness in their interviews. Their interests are an afterthought, and they concentrate on what's in it for the employer. This selflessness is what gets top candidates hired the fastest.

The Seamless COO, Danielle Demming and I have interviewed thousands of people for every position you can think of: sales, marketing, customer success, engineering, you name it. And the people that we always love to hire are the ones who do a great job of highlighting the value, the results, and the impact they can make for Seamless.

They come to the interview with actual strategies to help us win new customers. They come in with ideas to develop a better product, and recommendations for how we can build an unstoppable culture.

The strongest candidates don't come in saying, "I need X base," "I need Y benefits," or "What are you gonna do for me, me, me?" In fact, they hardly say "I" and "me." Instead, they're all about what they can do for our people and our customers to take the organization to the next level.

That's exactly the mindset and thought process you need to have in your interview.

What are you going to do for this employer if they hire you?

As a sales candidate, before you have your interview, come up with a list of ideas, strategies, and recommendations, to help the company's sales, grow their pipeline, or shorten their sales process.

What pains does the sales team have and how can you solve that?

Bring in ideas about how the product could be better. Share industry knowledge or white papers that could help propel the business forward.

It's all about Value, Value, Value.

Here are some examples of ways job candidates have brought value to Seamless during their interview process:

- Do sample work for free. One of my top employees at Seamless, Mason Johnson, sliced up old YouTube content I had and created videos that we could use to promote the company on social media. Not only did we hire him, but he's one of the first 15 employees at the company.

- Create sales lead lists of companies/prospects that you could sell to.

- Create cold email scripts.

- Pitch the company to other people/companies.

- Create a video and post it to social media about why you want to work at this organization.

- Send a custom video to every hiring manager and leader at the company on the value you can provide.

- Identify a potential problem within the company and create a solution.

- During the interview lay out what you would be able to accomplish for the first 30/60/90 days.

- Identify competitors and be able to articulate the core differences between the competitors and the company you're applying to.

- Remember **WIIFTE**: What's In It For The Employer?

Place WIIFTE at the front of your mind when you're in your interview. Focus every answer on how you can benefit the company, and come up with creative ways that you can show WIIFTE during the interview.

When you put the company first, you win!

WORK FOR FREE IF YOU HAVE TO

Let's say that you apply to one of your dream companies, you follow all the steps I've outlined in this book, and for some reason, things don't work out, and they decide to go with another candidate. This is a hard pill to swallow, but from time to time it does happen– it's an inevitable reality in today's job market.

What would you do?

If you think that thanking them for their time and moving on to the next job opportunity is the best move to make, you're wrong.

One of the best ways to get that dream tech sales job is to make an offer to work for them for free.

You can tell them that you are SO confident in your abilities, you will work for free for 30 days.

If you can't do 30 days free then do 14 days free, whatever your availability is.

I know this is controversial advice, and in today's economy, no one wants to work for free. I get that. However, if this is a company that you've dreamed about, and if you think the returns you can get from this job are going to far outweigh the few weeks you spend working for free, I would highly advise you to take the leap and do it.

If you desperately want to work for a company, you have to do whatever it takes to get the job. And sometimes that means doing some work for free.

Keep in mind as well that when I say "free work," it doesn't necessarily mean clocking in. It can be prospecting, appointment setting, or even referring people in your network to the product or services.

When I interview potential job candidates who have built free sales lead lists, written reviews about our products, bought and read our books, wrote sample email scripts, or created a video pitching our brand... If I had any doubts about the candidate before, making this extra effort wins me over every time.

Going the extra mile like this doesn't just show me what a great fit you will be at my organization, but it also lets the employer know just how tenacious you are. That even when you're faced with rejection, you still make a Hail Mary pass to make your dreams a reality. That type of grit can't be taught, and it's invaluable in a sales job candidate.

It's interesting that in the past few years, we'll get some job applicants who will have an attitude if we ask them to send in sample work as a part of the interview process. They'll get huffy and just say "No."

But when you take into account the employer's perspective. When you have so many applicants who look alike with the same experience and skills. Sample work is the one way you can evaluate the potential of one candidate over another.

At times, the only way you're going to stand out is if you put some skin in the game and show the HR team what you can do with sample work.

The more you give, the more you get in life.

Free work is how I was able to build a $1,000,000,000 company like Seamless in less than three years.

We give every user hundreds of dollars in credits for free for joining Seamless.AI when we could be charging thousands right from the start.

We spend nearly $250,000 a month creating free content for our newsletter, our podcast, and all our social media platforms.

I spend years on book projects that help people generate six and seven figures in sales, and I only charge $10-20 for the book.

The more you give to the people you serve without expecting anything in return, the more your life changes for the better.

This is one of the greatest secrets to sales and it's a fundamental principle for long-term success.

PART 10

THE TRAINING

W hether you know it or not, salespeople are just like professional athletes. As a professional athlete, you have to train every day to become the best you can be. Some of my favorite athletes are Tom Brady, LeBron James, and Steph Curry. These athletes train and practice every day to become the best that they can be.

They work out every day.

They eat healthy every day.

They practice offensive plays every day.

They practice defensive plays every day.

And they study game films every day.

As someone looking to get a job in tech sales and make $100,000 per year or more... you need to train every day too.

YOU NEED TO PRACTICE YOUR OFFENSIVE PLAYS:

- Build sales lists to book interview meetings

- Cold email for jobs

- Cold call for jobs

- Social sell on LinkedIn for jobs

- Video message for jobs

- Book interviews

- Attend interviews

- Write follow-up messages after interviews

- Read books on sales

- Read books on job hunting

YOU NEED TO PRACTICE YOUR DEFENSIVE PLAYS:

- Write interview Q&A scripts

- Roleplay

- Practice pitching a prospective employer

- Practice if an interviewer says, "Cold call me right now"

- Practice if an interviewer says, "Cold email me right now"

- Practice if an interviewer says, "Why should I hire you vs the other 100 applicants?"

- Practice FAQs an interviewer would ask

In addition to your offensive and defensive plays, you need to practice mental toughness and master the mindset principles and habits in the book, *Whatever It Takes* (one of our bonuses for writing a review) to achieve success no matter what.

You need to learn that success in life requires extreme ownership of everything good and bad. So never forget that you are not a victim. You are where you are because of you and no one else. If you achieve success, it's because of you. And if you don't achieve success, it's because of you.

Your goal should be to train and improve at least 1% every day as a job seeker and as a salesperson when you land your dream job.

I'm proof of the value of training every day. Growing up I was an average kid in school, no smarter or better off than you, and I could barely sit still and concentrate on anything.

The only reason I've been able to achieve this level of success is because I do whatever it takes and train every day like a professional sales athlete prepping to win The Super Bowl.

You need to do the same.

You can go from broke to financially free regardless of your background or education in tech sales if you train every day.

PART 11

THE OFFER

C ongratulations! You've accomplished 95% of the work you need to get a job in tech sales and make $100,000 a year!!!

I'm so happy for you and so damn proud of you.

Now when you finally get offers for tech sales jobs, I want to give you some advice to help save you from the mistake a lot of salespeople make.

When a lot of candidates get an offer, they get a bit ahead of themselves and just select the company with the highest paying salary.

This is the biggest mistake you can make when reviewing job offers.

Your #1 priority when you get a job offer should be to get into the dream company that you want to sell for the next few years.

Even if the salary is lower, most likely the On-Target Earnings (OTE) / Benefits / Education / Mentorship is much higher.

Don't overthink the salary, the benefits, and the commissions, and do all kinds of overly complicated math to split hairs about these things.

- Is it a great salary?

- Is it a great commission structure?

- Is it a product and a company you would love to sell for?

- Is there opportunity for promotion?

- Is there unlimited commission-earning potential?

- Did you have a great time meeting the individuals on the team?

If you answered "Yes" to all these questions, then you should say "Yes" to the offer.

The reason I say this is because when you're in sales, the base salary is the lower priority factor you should worry about.

The way I became a millionaire in tech sales was by taking a job that had a lower salary but an amazing commission model with uncapped commissions.

As long as you have a great product, unlimited commissions, and great leadership to learn from... you will win.

I went from taking a job making $40,000 to $50,000 a year as a base salary with unlimited commissions to now being worth over $100,000,000. Comparing $5k - $10k base salaries does not matter, trust me!

When you review an offer, run through the Six-Figure Sales Math. If there's opportunity to generate six figures in sales, take the offer and get kick-started on your new tech sales career. You never want to step on millions to pick up pennies. In other words, don't take a job at a shitty company with a terrible product because you can make $5k - $10k more with the base salary.

When you sign on to work for a company like that, guess what happens? You can't sell the product to anyone because it's terrible. You aren't passionate about the company, the product, or the target customers. You never get promoted because you can't sell. You wake up every day going into a miserable dead-end job. You don't learn or grow because you don't have any support or training.

Let's say a company growing 10% a year is offering you an SDR job at a $60K base / $40k commission, but this organization only has 100 employees, it's growing at a turtle's pace, the product is terrible, and the culture is toxic.

You might take that job because the base salary is more appealing, but I promise you, you'll be miserable every day.

More importantly, if the product is bad, that higher base salary might be all you make in a year which would be the worst scenario possible.

By contrast, if you have an opportunity to work at a high-growth company with a great base, an amazing commission structure, an incredible product, training, support, promotion, career growth, etc.... the world is yours!

For example, our base salary at Seamless for entry-level salespeople is $40k - $50k with $50k - $60k commissions. On top of this, we've got an amazing product, hundreds of internal training courses, amazing benefits, incredible PTO, Summer Fridays off, unlimited promotion, and career trajectory tracks.

I've literally seen interns at Seamless go from an intern's salary of $10 / hour to making $500,000 a year in less than three years because that's just how amazing our product, training, and customers are.

When you are in the right vehicle with the right team selling the right product like Seamless, you will win and you will maximize your success.

So when you're evaluating offers, play the long game instead of the short game. Think about the long-term returns you can generate when the product, the company, and the growth potential all come together in alignment.

When you find a company that will do whatever it takes to maximize your success, take their offer because you will have an opportunity of a lifetime.

Once you have selected a job offer to move forward with, come back because we'll share with you the tips you need to make sure you knock your first 90 days at your tech job out of the park!

PART 12

YOUR FIRST 90 DAYS

C ongratulations! You have accepted an offer and now it's time to finally get to work at your new tech job.

The greatest advantage that you have in your first 90 days is this book and my team as partners to help you exceed your goals.

Since you've studied and executed everything I've shared with you, you're likely starting as a Sales Development Rep (SDR), a Business Development Rep (BDR), or an Inside Sales Rep (ISR). This means you are prospecting, pitching, and closing appointments for your sales team around the clock.

But (and this is the greatest part about working an entry-level sales job), you get to cut your teeth and make $100,000 a year without even knowing how to close sales…

All you have to do is learn how to pitch ideal customers on why they should take a demo or discovery call to learn more about your software.

And once you book the appointment, your account executives will demo that prospective customer and work the opportunity to closed won or closed lost.

The benefits of working an entry-level job in tech sales are endless, but there is also plenty of training involved. To be a truly great SDR, you will need the following…

- You will need to know how to use the #1 list-building & appointment-setting software, Seamless.AI.

- You will need to know how to use a CRM all day to keep track of your leads.

- You will need to know how to make cold calls, emails, and social contacts to book appointments.

- You will need to know how to prospect, pitch, and close people on booking demos with you.

- Lastly, you will need to develop a sales funnel and reverse engineer your quota so you know exactly what sales activity to crush every day to be successful.

Do any of these objectives look familiar? They should, because if you've diligently been reading *The Ultimate Guide To Breaking Into Tech Sales*, then you've already familiarized yourself with these tasks, and you're ready to hit the ground running in your first 90 days.

The only extra training you will likely have to pick up is the organization's software product, their custom sales process, and the sales technology stack they use. But in all honesty, more than half the hard work is already done at this point. The rest should be a breeze, which is great news.

Congrats and cheers to being proactive with your sales career!

My final recommendations for you on your first 90 days are the following:

BE POSITIVE

Have a zero-tolerance policy for negativity. When you face obstacles or challenges (this is inevitable with every career, no matter the industry or your seniority level), find the good in the situation and look for a solution. Companies love positive employees, and they love to promote people who multiply the culture and the success of the organization. By contrast, the employees who are negative and toxic get fired fast because they kill the culture and productivity of their team. So get into the habit of always looking at the glass as half-full.

BE COACHABLE

No matter how far you climb in your organization, how much you make, what you learn, or how well you perform… you have to stay humble and coachable.

Do what your managers tell you to do and say what your leaders tell you to say.

A majority of my success is not because I was smart or talented, but because I took advice seriously, and I was always the most hungry, humble, and hard-working person in the room.

Coachability is all about admitting you don't know everything and consequently being hungry to improve 1% every day.

WORK HARD

Work as hard as you possibly can.

The trick that I used when I sold for IBM and Google was to take whatever my quota was and multiply that goal marker by 3x-5x. Then I just reverse-engineered the activity I needed to hit the 5x goal.

By putting in more work and effort than your peers, you will hit the 3x, 4x or maybe even 5x goal number, earn the #1 spot on the leaderboard, and destroy your sales quota.

Always maximize your goals and reverse-engineer the daily sales activity.

DO WHATEVER IT TAKES

I've worked with thousands of salespeople at Seamless.AI, and all the most successful people had this principle in common: WIT or Whatever It Takes.

They all had the grit to do Whatever It Takes to get the job, to maximize their success, their company's success, and their customers' success. These individuals assumed 100% ownership in their successes or failures, they never blamed others, and they never played the victim game.

Take ownership of your career and always be willing to do Whatever It Takes.

These are just a few secrets to crushing your first 90 days. To unlock all the cheat codes to success, make sure you get a copy of my #1 bestselling book, *Whatever It Takes*. It's completely free if you leave a review of *The Ultimate Guide To Breaking Into Tech Sales* on Amazon, screenshot it, and send it to:

www.BrandonBornancin.com/techsalesbonus

Whether you know it or not, your mindset, your perspective, and what you believe you're capable of will make or break you in tech sales. *Whatever It Takes* gives you the bulletproof mindset and operating principles to become unstoppable at any company, no matter the product you sell, or the state of the economy and the market. So write a review, pick up *Whatever It Takes*, and study it from cover to cover!

Lastly, there are a lot of books out there that are non-sales related but can show you the blueprint for how to hit the ground running during your first 90 days on the job.

I urge you to check out some of these books because they can provide useful insight into more general organizational and workflow strategies that play a part in you becoming a top performer on your sales team right away.

Here are two of my top recommendations:

- **Michael D. Watkins' *The First 90 Days: Proven Strategies for Getting***

Up to Speed Faster and Smarter

In Watkins' *The First 90 Days*, he'll show you how you can make an impact right away at your organization (no wasting time with onboarding and busy work), and how to diagnose your performance to ensure that you are on track to becoming a top performer ASAP.

- **Brian P. Moran's *The 12 Week Year: Get More Done in 12 Weeks Than Others Do in 12 Months***

If you think you can achieve something in a year, you'll take a year to get it done. If you think you can achieve something in 12 weeks, you'll crush it in just 12 weeks.

If you believe it, you can achieve it. Moran's *12 Week Year* puts this saying to practice as he breaks down tips on how to squeeze the urgency out of your first 90 days.

In addition to my top two recommendations, any top-rated books on Amazon about maximizing your success in the first 90 days on the job are great as well. Search Amazon and pick any up on this topic if you feel you still need more info to hit the ground running!

You made it!

You should be so proud of how far you've come, and I want to wish you good luck with your first job in tech sales! The tech sales community is going to be 10x stronger and better because of amazingly talented people like you!

As you transform your customers' lives forever and for the better by introducing them to groundbreaking products, never forget that with grit, dedication, and consistent hard work you can crush it in sales, positively impact lives, and achieve financial freedom for yourself.

The Seamless team and I can't wait for you to freaking kill it!

CONCLUSION

C ongratulations on finishing *The Ultimate Guide To Breaking Into Tech Sales!*

Tech sales is the greatest job in the world, and I need you to join the movement and be a part of it. It will change your life forever, just like it has for me and millions of other top tech sales professionals. This career will provide you with the highest amount of money, time, freedom, benefits, uncapped earning potential, and happiness you deserve, all from working out of the comfort of your own home.

I became financially free in tech sales by using the secrets in this book as the foundation to make it happen.

Tens of thousands of President's Club Winners at: **www.Presidents-ClubAwards.com** have also made over $100,000 and over $1,000,000 doing the same.

If they can do it, I need you to believe that you can do it too!

To get a job in tech sales, make over $100,000+ per year, and win our famous President's Club Award, all you need to do is study, execute, optimize, and repeat everything you've learned in this book.

It's not easy, but I promise you it will be worth it.

Let me repeat that so it really sinks in… I want you to listen here and take massive action to change the trajectory of your life forever for the better.

Study and execute the secrets that I laid out in this book step-by-step every day until you get a job in tech sales and make over $100,000 / year!

The most successful tech salespeople I know who read this book had faith that this process works. They launched their job search campaigns, wrote their scripts, practiced their interview questions, and mastered how to evaluate offers without any hesitation.

They didn't overthink it, they didn't question the strategies, and they didn't doubt the advice.

They just did whatever it takes, set big goals, took massive action, executed the secrets, tracked their performance, worked to beat their past results every week, and started generating big results as quickly as the first few days.

Never forget that sales is a profession where you get what you put in.

If you put in minimum effort, then you'll barely get any results.

If you don't apply the secrets…

If you don't build the lists and prospect the lists every day…

If you don't work on daily, consistent improvement…

You won't ever generate the results you want.

However, if you continue to do whatever it takes in sales to serve your customers, your company, and your family at the highest level. If you continue to put in the effort, the drive, the focus, the attitude, the positivity, the coachability, and the hard work, the sales activity… The sky's the limit.

If you practice every day to get just a little bit better than who you were and where you were the day before – your sales will increase, opportunities will increase, and your success will multiply like wildfire.

That's the beauty of sales, and there's nothing else like it on the planet!

My life's mission is to help you go from broke to financially free. And the best vehicle for me to help you do that is to inspire you to get your dream job in tech sales now!

Not only should you want to do this for yourself, but the world is counting on you and needs you to be successful.

I need you to be successful.

Your family needs you to be successful.

Your dreams are dying for you to become successful.

So leverage everything I taught you in this book and make your goals a reality.

Additionally, when you get your tech sales job, please post about it on Amazon reviews for *The Ultimate Guide To Breaking Into Tech Sales*. The reviews mean the world to me and our team who poured our hearts and souls into helping you with this book. You can drop a review here:

www.BrandonBornancin.com/techsalesbonus

You can also write a post on LinkedIn about how this book helped you get a job in tech sales. I love seeing readers and fans post selfies with my books. Tag me on LinkedIn with a picture or post on *The Ultimate Guide To Breaking Into Tech Sales* so I can celebrate with you! Here is my link:

www.linkedin.com/in/BrandonBornancin

Your success is our success and it truly fuels our fire. We have a gong in our office that my team and I bang loudly every single time we help someone get into tech sales. I need you to be our next GONG hit!

Lastly, I want you to land your dream job in tech sales so I can help you win our famous President's Club Awards at:

www.PresidentsClubAwards.com

When you make over $100,000 in sales, I'll ship you your custom Six Figure President's Club Award.

And when you make over $1,000,000 in sales, I'll ship you your custom Seven Figure President's Club Award. This is the ultimate award, our platinum money makers' trophy.

Our mission at Seamless.AI is to help 1,000,000 salespeople make over

$1,000,000 in sales and win our famous Seven Figure Club Award.

When you make over $100,000 or $1,000,000 in sales, apply for your custom President's Club Award at:

www.PresidentsClubAwards.com

Lastly, I love networking, coaching, and hanging out with top salespeople (your network is your net worth after all). So don't be a stranger!

CONNECT AND SUBSCRIBE WHERE I POST DAILY SALES SECRETS BELOW:

- **Website:** www.BrandonBornancin.com

- **LinkedIn:** www.linkedin.com/in/BrandonBornancin

- **Podcast:** www.apple.co/3FDG4y0

- **YouTube:** www.youtube.com/seamlesscontacts

- **Instagram:** www.instagram.com/BrandonBornancinOfficial

- **Newsletter:** www.seamless.ai/about/blog

- **Email:** brandon@seamlessai.com

- **Twitter:** www.twitter.com/SeamlessAI

- **Facebook:** www.facebook.com/BrandonBornancinOfficial

You can also download my digital business card and contact info at **www.BrandonBornancin.com**.

Congrats again on finishing *The Ultimate Guide To Breaking Into Tech Sales!*

Welcome to the greatest job in the world. Go make it happen, "Whatever It Takes!"

We Are Hiring

Seamless.AI has over 500 open sales positions.
Apply Today at Seamless.AI/Careers!

Join Our Team

seamless.AI/careers

Apply Now

GIVE TO GET BY SERVING OTHERS

Before you start the most incredible chapter of your life in tech sales, consider writing a review:

www.amzn.to/3Yki4qT

There are plenty of people out there who are right where you were when you started this book. Completely unaware of all their talents and unsure of what to do after college or how to thrive during these tough economic times.

Your review is going to help these people learn about *The Ultimate Guide To Breaking Into Tech Sales* and start their own journey to success.

Plus, when you write a review, screenshot it, and upload it at:

www.BrandonBornancin.com/techsalesbonus

We will grant you access to our bonus bundle…

Write a Book Review & Get
Over $1,935 in Bonuses!

Claim your FREE Bonus Bundle

EVERYTHING YOU'RE GOING TO GET:

- Unlock *Whatever It Takes* – The ultimate guide to building top sales habits, eliminating the bad ones, and maximizing your success in tech sales, relationships, and life! (Value $29.97)

- Get **Seamless.AI** – The #1 sales software to find cell phones, emails, and direct dials for anyone using artificial intelligence. Over $250 Credits Free! (Value $250)

- Get your very own **Tech Sales Earnings Calculator** – The only tool you need to easily calculate your path to earning $100K in tech sales FAST! (Value $147)

- Get **The Big 150 HR List** HR People Don't Want You To Have! This list includes 150+ Titles for every HR and recruiting title you need to prospect so you book more interviews and get in… (Value $257)

- Crush your goals, book more interviews than ever before and sign that dream job offer sooner than later with the help of our behind the scenes **Sales Activity Tracker!** (Value $147)

- Full access to the **Sales Secrets Master Class** – Over 100+ hours of exclusive interviews where the world's top sales experts reveal their secrets to success (Value $597)

- Get **Contact & Company Intelligence** – 50+ data points to personalize your outreach to recruiters and hiring managers, cut through the noise, and flood your calendar with job interviews (Value $207)

- Unlock the **Special Scripts Bonus** that includes 20 extra plug-and-play scripts you can use to connect with recruiters and hiring managers for every channel (from email to social) (Value $97)

- Immediate access to the **Job Offer Scoring Checklist** – A foolproof scoresheet to evaluate and compare your offers so you choose the job that's the perfect fit for you! (Value $107)

- Instant access to **The Top Secret Interview Questions**. Over 20+ of the most common tech sales interview questions that no one tells you to prepare for. Learn how to answer these to stack up the job offers!!! (Value $97)

Scan to Write a Review & Claim Bonuses!

Total Value: $1,935

www.BrandonBornancin.com/techsalesbonus

Made in the USA
Monee, IL
10 February 2023

8ecc1f4b-add8-44a4-9ff2-bf28d0f969e3R01